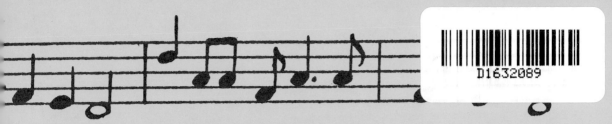

st for all.
eave the rest.. Strive for the high-est our mot - to bold,

o-claim it on high, Quae-ri-te Summa Our school's bat-tle cry.

Great Days and Jolly Days

The story of girls' school songs

HODDER AND STOUGHTON
London . Sydney . Auckland . Toronto

Great Days and Jolly Days

by CELIA HADDON

Title page: the girls of Bentley Friary Girls' School, Hertfordshire, in 1917.

Acknowledgements

This book is dedicated to the hundreds of old girls who have helped me write it. On the pages that follow they will recognise their work—the songs recalled, the memories, and the insights into days past. I must also thank the many heads and principals who allowed me to use their schools' songs and helped me find the original authors. In their turn, these were all generous with help. The debt of thanks I owe is immense, to people all over the world. There are so many of them, indeed, that I cannot give their names. I have mentioned people merely when the context seemed to require it. There are hundreds more who helped. It is literally true that without their help this book could not have been written. It is, really, their book.

I have done my best to track down copyright holders. I have written to every school that I could trace but some have either closed down, moved or changed their names. If head teachers have asked me not to use their songs I have respected their wishes. But, as I know I have failed to find *everybody*, I have set aside a substantial proportion of the royalties to go to a charity connected with women.

I must specifically thank the Bedford College Union for allowing me to quote their college songs, Peter Newbolt for permission to use an extract from "The Best School of All" from *Poems New and Old* by Sir Henry Newbolt, published by John Murray, and the John Lewis Partnership, Bentalls Ltd, the New Zealand High Commission, the Educational Supply Association, the GPDST, Max Hoather and many individuals for the loan of pictures.

Contents

For, working days or holidays,
And glad or melancholy days,
They were great days and jolly days
At the best School of all.

                              Sir Henry Newbolt

Foreword

If your schooldays were a long time ago, as mine were, this book will remind you with a mixture of amusement, affection, and nostalgia tinged with gratitude, of a lot that is good to remember. It was easier being a child in those days. We had time to grow up in. Confidence, and a harmless sense of belonging and loyalty, were natural to us. Fair play and keenness were not despised. (I'm still fond of both.) It is easy to laugh at some of the songs and sentiments in this admirable collection: and I do. The world it represents was over-simplified and self-satisfied, but I refuse to feel guilty for having enjoyed being at school in the 1920s.

Some forty odd years ago, before I went into the theatre, Virginia Graham, former *Spectator* film critic and "V.G." of *Punch*, wrote the words and music of a pastiche school song for me to sing with her to amuse ourselves and our friends. I'd forgotten about it until I read Celia Haddon's well-researched and affectionate book. The accuracy of Virginia's song is proved to be pretty deadly.

> Here's to the girls of the dear old school
> Who follow through life its golden rule
> To sing and whistle no matter how it hurts,
> And never to forget St. Ethelbert's.
> Here's to the girls who have writ its name
> In letters of fire in the Halls of Fame,
> And here's to the others,
> Who lift their heads to listen
> When this song is sung.
> (*Into a minor key*)
> Here's to the girls who with torch in hand
> Have left their alma mater
> For a foreign land.
> (*Major again*)
> Where'ere they may be their hearts beat high
> Beneath the pink and yellow of the old school tie.

Chorus:
Gloriana Pons asinorum,
Hic, haec, hoc, ad nauseam.
Quid pro quo et multum in parvo,
Floreat St. Ethelbert's.

Great Days and Jolly Days is written with respect for the dedication that went into creating schools that tried and succeeded in producing women ready and able to cope with situations never imagined in the halcyon days when many of these songs were first sung. I'm glad about this. The book is full of enjoyable treasures. I particularly like athletic Kingsley, (page 61), but my favourite comes from Wimbledon House (later Roedean). This is the chorus:

Wimbledonia, fair are free,
Health and strength belong to thee.
Felix Wimbledonia.

As I read the book I remembered the feeling of real sadness on the day I left school. But I was also jolly glad to be rid of hockey, walking in a "croc", and the ill-fitting dark brown forage caps that we wore "cross-wise" and not fore-and-aft.

JOYCE GRENFELL

The Vanishing Songs 1

Most of us remember our schooldays, women perhaps a little more than men. Somehow memories seem to increase in clarity with age, as if the years brought us closer to our old selves. Forgetting the names of recent acquaintances, we can still remember Miss Chesterman the English mistress or Willy, Miss Williams, the games mistress. And with those thoughts of school come odd snatches of music, occasional lines or sometimes whole verses of a completely remembered school song. Have you, reader, forgotten yours? Probably not. It is lingering somewhere in the mind and needs only a jolt of memory to bring it, and its schoolgirl world, back to life.

"Here are the words of my school song," wrote an old girl to me, when I started trying to collect together girls' school songs. "It's extraordinary that I should remember them so clearly since I have never been to a reunion and am not given to reminiscences of schooldays." "The words are still fresh in my mind," wrote another, "and they bring a lump to my throat, after first singing it in 1935." While a girl of the sixties admitted: "It does strike me as rather odd that I can still sing the school song with no prompting but the Beatles' lyrics and tunes are only recalled in odd snatches."

In an age when conservationists are trying to preserve our old buildings, our beautiful landscapes and our wild creatures, few people have bothered to point out that we are losing our girls' school songs. They are dying out as surely as the glow-worms, or the large blue butterflies, or the sand snakes that cannot find a place to breed in the modern countryside. No body of conservationists is trying to save them. Very often, not even the schools bother. They will study local history, but forget their own past. Many school songs exist only in the memory of old girls, or in torn and tattered copies among the junk that means nothing except to its owner.

Ironically the songs themselves frequently speak of the permanence of the institutions they honour. Some time around 1929 Miss J. M. Abbott, headmistress of Leamington College for Girls, wrote a song for her school. She saw her work as the foundation of something enduring. She looked into the future with confidence.

As here we pass our time
Through wind and weather
O School, we build thy walls
By strong endeavour;
Planting a fadeless tree,
Blazing the pilgrim's way,
What can we bring to thee?
What shall we carry away?

Chorus
Faith in life's destiny,
Hope for the years to be,
Love that we bear to thee;
These we shall carry away.

Would she have written the same verse, if she'd known that 1977 was to see the end of Leamington College? Merged into a federation of schools, because of reorganisation, it is now a part of North Leamington School. What has happened to Leamington College has happened all over Britain. In the state system alone some 600 or more girls-only schools have disappeared in the last decade, and more will no doubt follow. It is the price of the swing towards comprehensive and co-educational schools. In private education, the enemy is inflation which is taking its toll of the less flourishing girls' schools. Those in favour of the changes see only the gains. They barely pause to regret the passing of old customs. And even when the change is not welcomed, it is accepted as part of the pattern of our time. Perhaps the most striking difference of all between those earlier generations and ourselves is that they expected their schools to last.

Chandos School, we here today
Sing what we mean to do and be,
To thee our formal vows we pay,
We lift our hearts and hands to thee.

Chorus
Chandos School! We'll live and strive
To keep thy honoured name alive.

That song was sent to me by a teacher who had spent nearly all her working life in Chandos School, Stanmore. "It was my good fortune to remain in the school throughout," wrote Miss R. Grimley, "rising to the position of deputy head and finally becoming its fourth headmistress. My own school opened in August 1939 and closed in July 1974, at that time combining with the boys' school to become a co-ed comprehensive high school."

Boarding school pupils can never forget those agonising station farewells. "I remember imploring my mother not to cry," recalls an old QASite (a girl from Queen Anne's School, Caversham.) "It used to be put down as 'wet' if you cried and my mother used to let me down only too often."

Even when the school survives, its song is often forgotten. "The enclosed song was sung at a tea party in Camberley four years ago held on the fiftieth anniversary of the hostess entering the hallowed portals of The Royal School, Bath," said the letter which accompanied this song:

Royal School! Our fathers lived and died for honour,
May we be as they were, loyal, brave and true,
Serving God and country, striving that upon her,
His blessing may descend, and all our zeal renew.
Royal School! Royal School!

"All the guests at the party were ex-Royal School," the letter continued. "The song was sung with great gusto by those of the 1920s vintage, but had never been heard before by those of the 1950s vintage. The chorus sounded very similar to the View Halloo of fox-hunting." In the same way Crayford School, in Kent, has entirely forgotten what was its song before the war. Even an earlier headmistress could not recall this:

> Amid green fields and fair orchards,
> Near Thames winding down to the sea,
> Crayford School has arisen,
> The Central School, healthy and free.
>
> We work with a will, we are earnest.
> At lessons and games one can see,
> Our utmost we do for the highest—
> Our aim till our life's end shall be.

Songs like this date fast, in some cases because the school name changes, in others, particularly the light-hearted ones, because sentiment changes. Thus, some schools have more than one song in their history. In 1887, still the time when founding schools for girls was a pioneering activity, Wigan had a girls' high school. In the first years of the century it acquired a rousing school song, written by Henry Brierley, chairman of the governing body, a great raconteur and a stout Lancastrian.

> Our brothers boast with conscious pride,
> Of Rugby, Harrow, Eton;
> And though it's true those schools are old,
> Our girls' school can't be beaten,
> Of Bedford High School's fame we hear,
> Of Cheltenham's school, a big one;
> But what of them? Today we greet
> The Girls' High School of Wigan.
>
> *Chorus*
> So all from Kindergarten
> Up to the Sixth,
> To our School be loyal and true.
> Our colours keep from stain,
> Uphold with might and main
> The honour of our school for aye.

"We loved it," recalls Betty Thompson, a 1927 to 1934 old girl. "But while I was there a headmistress abolished it on the grounds that it was doggerel." In 1945, after a competition, the English teacher, Miss

Hindshaw, produced a new song with less doggerel, but without the same Lancastrian ring to it. Moral endeavour succeeded local pride.

> Pilgrims we on life's highway,
> Journeying on unflagging ever,
> March we onward day by day,
> Pilgrims in a great endeavour.

It's not great poetry. Girls' school songs rarely are. Indeed, sometimes they're not even very clear in meaning. But for all their faults they *matter*. Why otherwise did the headmistress of Liverpool High School, one of the Girls' Public Day School Trust foundations, insist on her school being known as the Belvedere School. The GPDST history maintains that it was partly because there were so many high schools in the district but also "partly because 'Belvedere' was richer in potential rhymes (all the school songs were written after the change)".

Some school songs are not in this book, because of sensitivity on the part of headmistresses about their schools' reputation. "Although the song is not sung nowadays, there will be 'old girls' in the City who still remember it with affection and I should not like anyone to feel offended by references to it," wrote a Birmingham headmistress. At a public school, a headmistress confessed: "I find the subject of girls' school songs embarrassing. I would prefer it if the song were not mentioned." It was a song that dated back to before the war, old fashioned, certainly, but not ridiculous. Yet somehow the headmistresses felt their schools might be diminished if their songs (however far back) were mocked.

The fiercest champions of school songs are often the pupils. At St. James's School, West Malvern, the school song—just its first verse—is still sung. Written by Canon Anthony Deane, chaplain to the king before the war, it is a nostalgic composition.

> High on the hill is the School we belong to—
> Old girls and present girls, answer the call!
> Dear is the home we are lifting our song to!
> Proudly we name it the best of them all!
> People of other schools, grant us your pardon,
> What we can show you for pride will atone;
> Archway and hockey-ground, cloister and garden—
> This is the place that we reckon our own!
>
> *Chorus*
> We shall remember it still!
> Ever the dearest of names,
> Here's to the School of St. James!
> Here's to our home on the hill!

The headmistress, Rachel Braithwaite, explained: "I, in fact, think it is very out of date but the girls still seem to like it, and so it continues to be used."

At Newport Priory Secondary Girls' School, Isle of Wight, the Head of Science, Oliver Frazer, wrote the school hymn in 1956. It was sung until 1970 when the school was reorganised. Five years later Mr. Frazer was touched to receive a letter from an old girl, who wrote asking permission to use the school hymn at her forthcoming wedding. At that great occasion, this was sung:

> God will lead us, we will follow,
> Over rugged crags and down the hollow,
> Through the woods with darkness growing,
> Over rivers, swiftly flowing,
> Unafraid and hearts a-glowing,
> God will lead us home.

But school songs are not just for old girls, or for retired mistresses. Today, the old songs are part of a world that we have lost. It is a world made up of certainties—the certainties, for instance, of Miss Rainbird. Miss Rainbird was the headmistress of a little Church of England school, St. Saviour's, in Hitchin. It was a school founded by a reverend gentleman and run on such old-fashioned lines that Miss Rainbird was called "Governess". She wrote this school song:

> Sunny, Straight and Steady
> Is the motto of our School.
> Dear children, aye be ready
> To keep our golden rule.
>
> Give place where it is needed,
> Obedience where 'tis due.
> Make this old world better,
> For having sheltered you.

With the certainty, went a formality. At the Harley St. Girls' School in Bath, Miss Bessie Hawkins, B.A., wrote songs for occasions that needed marking. There was, for instance, the end-of-term hymn:

> We plead thy pardon for the wrong words spoken,
> The frequent failures of the term now past,
> Lessons neglected, resolutions broken,
> The putting pleasure first and duty last.

As remarkable as the formality, was the confidence to be found in the school songs—a sort of optimism that seems as unfashionable in 1977 as the mention of duty in Miss Hawkins' hymn. At Barcroft Girls'

Secondary School, Willenhall, West Midlands, on the first and last
day of term, this innocently jolly song was sung with great gusto:

> Keep on looking for the bright, bright skies,
> Keep on hoping that the sun will rise,
> Keep on singing when the whole world sighs
> And you'll get there in the morning.

Now, less than twenty years later, the school is closed, and the song
gone with it.

A sense of fun, oddly out of place for some reason today, is also
found in the old songs.

> Girls of Dereham School are we,
> Working each in her degree,
> This our life and this our day,
> Books and hockey, work and play.
>
> But if failure walk beside,
> Down-hearted we, and heavy-eyed?
> No! We'll always merry be
> And success we'll surely see.

Loyalty, too, was not mocked.

> There's many a school in Britain
> And schools beyond the sea,
> Where girls may be as happy
> As clever and as free;
> But one I know in Shropshire,
> In the dear old West Country—
> Not far away from Shrewsbury town—
> Is just the school for me

—sang the girls of Whitchurch High School.

"Nowadays one has to be very snide and astringent and see
through all the humbug and guff of being 'loyal' and 'giving of one's
best' and being 'proud of the school' and you'll think me a corny old
cow if I say that I believe it was better for us and society to have this
'noble lie'. It became true in a way, because we *did* do our best and we
did feel happy doing it. All the rally, rally, jolly hockey sticks stuff was
(provided one made fun of it sometimes) basically more wholesome
than being just as absolutely nasty and useless and casual as one's
nature at its nastiest," wrote Alison Adcock, an old girl from the
Abbey School, Reading.

Bracing efforts in the gymnasium of Wilton House School, Reading, a generation ago. Disciplined gym displays were a favourite form of Speech-Day entertainment then–sometimes they still are.

She had been at the school just before and during the war. For her generation and others after, it was perhaps a "noble lie". For an earlier one, it seemed extraordinarily like truth. Miss Frances Jane Dove, the founder headmistress of Wycombe Abbey and one of the first Girton students, truly believed that the serious education received in the new girls' public and high schools, and the equally important education of the playing fields would transform society. "The great work our schools are doing," wrote Miss Dove, "is the raising of the whole moral tone of women's lives: honesty, fair-play, and *esprit de corps* are taking the place of petty meanness and jealousy; if only every girl would go to school and stay there long enough to learn the corporate virtues, in two or three generations we should realise Utopia."

Education on the playing field of Putney County Secondary School for Girls around 1918.

Love for the School 2

In pursuit of the corporate virtues, thousands of schoolgirls have, upon prize-days and special occasions, solemnly sung about the moral uplift of football. Girls' schools have usually been warmer, more intimate places than boys' schools, but much of their structure and theory has been based upon the example of the really good schools in Victorian days, which were, with only a handful of exceptions, schools for boys. So it is that generations of girls all over Britain used to sing (and occasionally still do) this football chorus:

> Follow up! Follow up! Follow up!
> Till the field ring again and again
> With the tramp of the twenty-two men.
> Follow up! Follow up! Follow up!

The father of the school song was John Farmer, a music teacher at Harrow in the second half of the nineteenth century. He started a tradition of school singing, first with Latin songs, then—daringly—with English verses. After several songs with a fellow Harrow master, Edward Bowen (who wrote the words), Farmer produced "Forty Years On" in 1872. "The blend of religion and football caused uneasiness in certain circles and was only passed after meeting with the approval of Matthew Arnold," says a Harrow historian. In 1885 Farmer brought out a songbook, in which "Forty Years On" was included. The song was taken up by Miss Frances Mary Buss's famous school, the North London Collegiate, Doncaster High, Putney County Secondary, Worthing Girls' High, Walthamstow Central, Dartford Grammar, Central Newcastle High, Wolverhampton High, Stockport High and many others.

It is a mystery why it should have caught on. As Miss Dove, of Wycombe Abbey, regretfully admitted, football was "quite out of the question on account of its roughness" for girls' schools. Yet this odd mixture of muscular Christianity and football was quite often sung without any change in the wording whatsoever. The chorus with its

Even girls' school architecture seemed to be influenced by the boys' public-school tradition. Putney County Secondary School with its tower and dome was a case in point.

"twenty-two men", of course, is the most strikingly unsuitable passage. Some other parts of the song might, after all, refer to hockey or lacrosse.

> Forty years on, growing older and older,
> Shorter in wind as in memory long,
> Feeble of foot and rheumatic of shoulder,
> What will it help you that once you were strong?
> God gave us bases to guard or beleaguer,
> Games to play out whether earnest or fun;
> Fights for the fearless and goals for the eager,
> Twenty and thirty and forty years on!

Nor is "Forty Years On" the only example of girls' schools happily singing boys' songs. King Edward VI Grammar School for Girls, Camp Hill, Birmingham, sings one that comes from the boys' school of the same foundation. It's a particularly rousing song, which I have heard sung with great panache by the school choir.

> Where the iron heart of England
> Throbs beneath its sombre robe,
> Stands a School whose sons have made her
> Great and famous round the globe;
> These have plucked the bays of battle,
> Those have won the Scholar's crown;
> Old Edwardians, young Edwardians
> Forward for the School's renown.
>
> *Chorus*
> Forward where the knocks are hardest,
> Some to failure, some to fame;
> Never mind the cheers or hooting,
> Keep your head and play the game.

*Young Edwardians
from Camp Hill,
Birmingham in 1919.
"We wore gym tunics
made of navy blue
serge with velvet yokes
and white winseyette
blouses," recalls Mrs.
Margaret Hewson (the
girl in the centre).
"My schooldays were
extremely happy."*

Another major influence in girls' schools songs was that of Girton College, Cambridge. Other colleges like Westfield, Bedford, and St. Mary's, Durham, have had their college songs; but Girton's were still in use when this book was written. (Now the College has decided to go co-educational, the future of its songs must be in doubt.) The songbook, brought out yearly for the College feast, starts with "Gaudeamus Igitur", the well-known Latin triumphal song which was originally sung when the first Girton students passed their Tripos exams in 1872. This has been used as a school song by schools such as Withington Girls' School, Manchester.

After the Latin start, the next sixteen songs (written on and off up to 1968) go into English. The one which best sums up the attitude of those first undergraduates—whose only lectures were given them by kindly dons in their spare time—was written in those first years when Girton College was still just a smallish rented house in Hitchin.

> Some talk of Senior Wranglers
> And some of Double Firsts,
> And truly of their species
> These are not the worst;
> But of all the Cambridge heroes
> There's none that can compare
> With Woodhead, Cook and Lumsden,
> The Girton Pioneers.

Sarah Woodhead, a grocer's daughter, Rachel Cook, from a professor's family, and Louise Lumsden were thus immortalised to the tune of "The British Grenadiers", as the first students to pass the Tripos exam.

From Girton a stream of "certificated students" (though allowed, under sufferance, to sit their Tripos exams, they were not allowed Cambridge degrees) issued into the new girls' high schools which, under the influence of pioneer headmistresses, were being founded all over Britain. Something of their progress can be measured by the song collections that sprang up in imitation of Girton—at St. Andrew's and at Wycombe Abbey in the steps of old Girtonian Frances Dove, at the now co-educational Westfield College where the first principal Constance Maynard came from Girton, and at Kingsley School, Sussex, where the collection included a song called "The Kingsley Pioneer". It was a far from easy life for these young women, conscious of the prejudice against them, often far from generously paid, and subject to extremely strict rules in the schools where they worked. But they brought with them high ideals and a great pride in their education. Their college gowns, symbols of the educational emancipation of women, were worn with touching pride on all occasions.

Gowns were de rigueur *even in the staff room at Blyth Secondary School, Norfolk, in 1936.*

*An early pioneer of
degrees for girls was
Miss E. Garbutt, the
first Headmistress of
Leeds Modern School
(now the Lawnswood
School). Miss Garbutt
had a degree from
London University
and disdained the title
of Head Governess,
which had been used
by her predecessor.
The school, first
known as the Ladies'
Educational Institute,
was one of the earliest
foundations when it
opened in 1854.*

The Mistress of Westfield, Constance Maynard, wrote one of the College's twenty-four songs on this theme of life outside College. Sung to "The Minstrel Boy", it goes:

> The new B.A. to her school has gone;
> In the ranks of a staff you'll find her.
> Her cap and gown she hath girded on,
> And her silk hood slung behind her.
> "College mine," said the dauntless maid,
> "Though all the world neglect thee,
> "One heart at least thy rights shall guard,
> "One faithful heart protect thee."

> The maiden worked; but the mark book's score
> Left her soul no time for dreaming;
> Old times she treasured more and more,
> In her mem'ry's mirror gleaming.
> She said, "Thy songs still come to me,
> "Oh home of love and bravery,
> "I'll work with the heart of the strong and free,
> "And not in a drudging slavery."

Despite all the drudging slavery of mark books, it is clear from the school songs all over the country that many of the first and subsequent mistresses continued to dream. One of the cruellest jokes of time is that when most people think of those two great pioneers (too early even for Girton), the headmistress of the North London Collegiate School and the headmistress of Cheltenham Ladies' College, they think in terms of a vulgar little rhyme.

> Miss Buss and Miss Beale,
> Cupid's darts do not feel.
> How different from us,
> Miss Beale and Miss Buss.

Yet nothing could have been farther from the truth. Both of these women were driven by passion, a passion for the education of girls and for their own particular schools.

The heart of the English school mistress has usually been filled with this great love. Many school songs, indeed, are love poetry—to the school. At the beginning of the 1930s Miss Margery Chambers became the founding headmistress of Wirral County Grammar School for Girls. She chose for motto: *Monumentum Aere Perennius* (meaning "a monument more lasting than grass") and for symbol Pharos, the lighthouse at Alexandria. "If I remember aright," recalls

*For the school
prospectus in about
1918, the
Headmistress of
Putney County
Secondary School
chose this pose–her
BA gown and mark
books well in evidence.*

an old girl, "the city of Alexandria could be defended by a flame from
the lighthouse directed onto enemy ships." Miss Chambers' school
song evokes the city and rings with a Biblical emotion.

Four-square it stands,
Like the new Jerusalem
Built on a rock,
Like the house in the parable
To endure through seventeen centuries,
Warden of the City,
Watcher of her Seas.

Lit by a flare which conquers distance
And penetrates the farthest ice-bound sea;
Armed with the pow'r to concentrate the flame
To burn her enemies,
Endowed with voice to utter warning.

So may we
Founded upon a rock,
Lit by a flaring passion for humanity—
Cry out against the wrongs of injustice and violence,
And armed with the burning power of love,
Defend the city.

The love affair between school and mistress was not always so stern. Quieter and more lyrical songs abound. Like the romantic poets before them, many school song writers have found their inspiration in the surrounding landscape. Miss Evelyn Hart, a mistress at the South Wilts Grammar School before the war, looked to the nearby Stonehenge and Salisbury Cathedral, and to the five rivers on the school badge, for her theme:

> Stronger than the storm swept stones
> Sounds the call of duty.
> Higher than the highest spire
> Leads the quest for beauty.
> To this school the task has come,
> Caught our youth and laughter,
> That a greater heritage
> We bequeath hereafter.
>
> *Chorus*
> Silver yet the five streams flow,
> Fails the green plain never,
> As from age to age we go,
> ONWARD, ONWARD ever.

In Kent, it was again a river that provided inspiration for the song of Rochester Grammar School. At the turn of the century Constance Ashford, probably a school mistress, wrote:

> Down in Kent! Oh, down in Kent!
> There's a river slow and wide,
> Barges with their red sails set,
> Drifting seaward down the tide.
>
> Down in Kent! Oh, down in Kent!
> There's a School which we shall make
> Strong as tide in river pent
> Fit to fight for old truth's sake.

In Gainsborough High School, Lincolnshire, it was the Vikings, who had sailed up the River Trent, who inspired a song. The looting, rapine and ale-joy were ignored in favour of their more spiritual qualities of Courage, Gaiety and the Quiet Mind (the school motto):

> Bold was the Northman, the sea-loving Dane;
> Peril ne'er stayed Cnut, Guthrum or Swegn
> Heirs of their name and their spirit are we,
> So let us press forward with hearts brave and free.

ᗰargate

THE highest medical and other scientific authorities are unanimous in their testimony to the almost unrivalled healthiness of Margate. The town being situated at the corner of a promontory, and fronted by the sea on three sides, the air is full of life and vigour.

At Cliftonville, where Queen's School is located, the cliffs are from fifty to eighty feet high, and the district is the healthiest and most bracing in Margate.

In the matter of sunshine, so essential to health, especially of children, Margate is singularly well favoured.

High places, in this case the cliffs of Margate, had an attraction for school founders. This opening page of the Queen's School prospectus in the 1930s shows the emphasis its principal, Mrs. Ethel Walton, placed on girlhood health.

> Gay was the Northman, though peril might lower;
> Song was his refuge in wearisome hour;
> We too will vanquish dejection and fear
> With laughter and singing, and be of good cheer.

Hills and high places seemed always to be an inspiration. They feature in very many school songs. "Hills are associated with moral endeavour," suggested one of my correspondents. A more down-to-earth theory might be that hills literally provided drainage and sewerage advantages for siting large buildings, and that only after this came their superior moral qualities. In 1944, when Allerton High School moved to a new site, its headmistress, Miss Norah Henderson, asked the senior physical education mistress, Miss Audrey Wilmott, to provide a school song. Miss Wilmott obliged with this:

> Wind on the upland, sun and shadow,
> Larks in the sudden silence thrill;
> White gulls wheel over field and furrow,
> Allerton on the hill.

> These you offer us, wisdom, knowledge,
> Dreams and hopes that we may fulfil;
> Joy of achievement, friendly laughter,
> Allerton on the hill.

But the loving eye of a school's governor, and the local pride of the Fenlander, could do without hills for inspiration. In Wisbech, a past chairman of the county education committee, J. H. Dennis, made a virtue of the "soil which God left virgin", and wrote this for the high school:

> Let those who live midst mountains
> Dream dreams and seek in song
> A world of happy freedom
> Where right will vanquish wrong;
> They only see in visions,
> Through mists from day to day
> The goal, to which our fathers
> Long sought and found the way.

Occasionally, this attachment to school found outlet in a song that would be too emotional for today's taste. Possibly written by a founding headmistress, the school song of St. Anne's, a public school in Westmorland, has a tone of high romance out of date in 1977. It provides, I think, an interesting insight into the tone of those early schools. "Girlhood"—a sentimental concept today—was real to very many teachers and parents in those days.

> The mighty hills around us call through wistful blue,
> "Be the best you can in girlhood, diligent, sweet and true."
> "Oh do! Oh do!" the songbirds pipe from many a tree,
> "Oh try! Oh try!" the rippling lake lilts with silvery glee.
>
> When later we seek leisure with willing feet and fleet,
> The breezes blow more softly, the roses smell more sweet;
> And when dark night enfolds us, the stars their love watch keep,
> For it's home and kin we dream of, in gentle soothing sleep.

This is the language of Tennyson's *Maud.* Nor is the St. Anne's song the only example. Something of the *feeling* that could be experienced in a school came over in a letter I received from Miss Eveline Jenner, a senior mistress at St. Margaret's High School for Girls, Henleaze Park, Bristol. The school, which was run privately, is closed now, but it used to be set in a beautiful bit of parkland. "St. Margaret's Day is July 20th, so it was annually celebrated as the School's 'Great Day'. By that date most of us were feeling hot and tired after a long and exciting term. Therefore our thoughts turned to dreams of seaside and country holidays. We watched the bees rejoicing on the scent of the clover and the swallows high above us. Our sense of duty helped us not to give in. The trees inspired us to aim high."

The school song was in the same vein, again in the romantic language of Tennyson.

> Humming bees follow the scent of the clover,
> Summerward swallows are winging their flight,
> Luring, the sea whispers, "Come to the rover"
> Divers are bringing the hidden to light.
> So we may sip nectar from knowledge and beauty,
> Here in this honeyhive cluster of girls,
> Or, holding fast to the lifeline of duty,
> Draw from deep thinking its wonderful pearls.
>
> Tall trees around us seem ever aspiring,
> Calling us upward from slackness and fear,
> Bracing our courage when study is tiring,
> Whisp'ring success at the close of the year.
> Oh! Let us press onward with joy in our striving,
> Games that we play and the work that we do
> May build the future so quickly arriving,
> Life that is useful and noble and true.

"Tall trees around us seem ever aspiring"—at Caldecote Towers, Hertfordshire, they also provided support for hammocks. This photograph of girls lazing on a hot summer day comes from the school's prospectus just after the First World War.

There was an intimacy about some of the private schools in those days that, I think, goes a long way to explain the sentiment. Girls before the First World War and indeed for some years after, were not expected to be grown-up. It is difficult to remember today, when sixteen-year-olds frequently get married and eighteen-year-olds don't even need to elope to Gretna Green, that the middle-class girl was a child until well into her teens. Smaller schools, therefore, had often a family atmosphere. At Caldecote Towers, near Watford, (now a Catholic convent of a different name), Miss Tate and Miss Tanner who ran the school from 1908 kept school pets. Every year they produced a calendar with pictures of the dogs, cats, geese, ducklings or horses that roamed the grounds. There were riding lessons for the whole school. And on Miss Tanner's birthday there were cricket matches against the gardeners, who included among the junior staff Fred Streeter, later to become famous.

The intimate atmosphere had been established in the first years of the century when the school was run by Miss Medina Griffiths. She was a pioneer in her attitude to education (exams mattered) and in her personal appearance (she cropped her hair—a daring innovation). She also produced a hymnbook and a songbook, with all but a few of the words and accompaniments written by herself. One of the hymns she wrote for the school was called "Little Footsteps" and started with a verse that is unthinkable for the modern teenage pupil.

> Little footsteps hurrying onwards,
> Little hearts by planning stirred,
> As ye enter on life's future,
> Take this as your guiding word:
> "Fear thou not, but trust in Me,
> "As thy day thy strength shall be."

A riding lesson at Caldecote Towers in the days of Miss Tate and Miss Tanner—older girls side-saddle, of course.

Girls before the First World War were not allowed to grow up too fast. The girls in this early classroom have neatly brushed or plaited hair and clean pinafores. Today they would be wearing adult fashions and possibly even make-up.

Nor would today's new pupil, fresh from primary school, take kindly
to a school song that went:

> Little girl in your great new school,
> What do you find in its life and rule?
> There's much to hear and much to see,
> I love my new School and my School loves me.
> I'm happy as a lark and busy as a bee,
> In the School of the Ivy Green.

Yet this was the school song of the Croydon High School for Girls, a
GPDST foundation. It was written by Miss E. M. Leahy who became
headmistress in 1901, but by the end of the 1920s it was no longer
sung. Apart from the implication of the childishness of the new
pupil, perhaps the other aspect of particular interest is the assumption that not only does pupil love school, but (surely this could not
have been assumed of boys' schools of the period?) school loves
pupil.

The same gentleness and softness is found in the first verse of the
song, written by Enid Lynch, of the Bolling High School, a Bradford
girls' school founded in 1879.

> Dear school, to thee we owe this song of praise,
> For all thy love and care through girlhood days.
> That love, from thee derived, unto the end
> Shall seal the sacred bond 'twixt friend and friend.
>
> *Chorus*
> Forward and upward then
> May we forever press.
> Thus shall we prove to thee our love,
> And show our faithfulness.

Pupils, too, responded with loving school songs. Marjorie Rushton,
head girl of Burnley High School in 1935, wrote a song that apos-
trophised the school as a friend.

> We vow to thee, our school and friend,
> All that our hearts and minds can give.
> For thee we work and laugh and play,
> To thee we sing, for thee we live.
> O teach us truth and tenderness
> For we shall always love thee most.
> We ask to seek thy happiness,
> Thy cause and honour make our trust.

At Parkfields Cedars School in Derby, the song was composed by one of the pupils, Pem Banks, now Mrs. Gerard. "The words and the music were produced overnight and it certainly was not suggested to me by anyone," she writes. "Those were the days of 1947 when the school honour was not something to be mocked and when hard work was rewarded with 'honour marks'." The song was phased out when the school went comprehensive, but Mrs. Gerard was touched to hear that the last set of prefects to leave had insisted on singing it, even though it wasn't on the official going-down service.

> True to the end our school shall be
> As she has been of yore.
> We cherish her good name, and pray
> To keep it evermore.
> For those who worked and thought and planned
> To make her as she is,
> We lift our voice in thanks to God
> And give Him what is His.

Pyrrhic dance on the tennis court at Parkfields Cedars School—an entertainment for parents in the days before the school went comprehensive.

At Greenhead High School, Huddersfield, a similarly affectionate song was written by Peggy Madden, now Mrs. Sinker. "I can't remember if there was any competition," she explains, "but Miss Hill, the headmistress, asked for it, to take the place of the Harrow School song, 'Forty Years On'. She came from Harrow—perhaps that was why she wanted something of her own for the school."

We shall look back when we are here no more
Some memory or echo of a song
Will bring before us half-forgotten days,
Then all red-lettered as they fled along.

Breeze of the field, gleam of the sun
Well-remembered faces and laurels hardly won
Will be with us till our working days are done.

Above the turmoil of the breathless game,
Above the laughter and the song which never dies,
Above the quiet of unbroken work,
Oh! Let the cry of "Honour" ever rise.

The intimacy and affection between pupil and school, which is so characteristic of these school songs, finds its most moving expression in a song from the Grammar School for Girls, West Kirby, Wirral. Written by Miss M. A. Layne, the headmistress in the 1930s, it makes the motherly side of school and headmistress explicit.

Give you greeting, O my daughters, you whose race is just begun,
You with eyes that shine like morning, you shall well and truly run,
You are mine to shape and fashion, you are mine to love and tend,
You are mine to give you courage that you come to glorious end.

You shall go forth, O my daughters, eager-hearted, unafraid,
Not through life to be defeated, holding on, still undismayed.
And the victory shall leave you all the gentler that it's won,
And the long day's work shall find you all the stronger that it's done.

"Now in loneliness and grief," wrote an old girl who had just lost her husband, "I know how difficult 'holding on' can really be. I suppose children still sing the school song, but I wonder if any of them ever give a second thought to those inspiring words? I know they mean far more to me now than when I sang them in my youth."

Maths, Latin and Grit 3

The fervour and enthusiasm in girls' school songs is not really surprising, if we remember how new the schools were. Even now most of them are less than a century old—compared to the three or four centuries of existence that many boys' public and grammar schools have behind them. In the days of our grandmothers, girls' schools were daring, even shocking, educational upstarts. The existing small parlour boarding schools had been genteel affairs where young ladies learned to play the piano, do a little fine needlework, make polite conversation, and perhaps pick up a smattering of bad French and a few useless history dates. The very idea of girls learning arithmetic, science or Latin was a joke—or, if not a joke, then a horrifying example of decadent modernity. For the first generation of pupils at the new high schools, this kind of serious study was a thrilling innovation. Latin, maths and science, then, find their way into girls' school songs—not because they are dreary compulsory subjects, but because they are exciting and daring new ideas.

In 1864 the Schools' Inquiry Commission was appointed by the Government to look at both boys' and girls' education, and concluded, "It cannot be denied that the picture brought before us of the state of Middle-Class Female Education is, on the whole, unfavourable. Want of thoroughness and foundation; want of system; slovenliness and showy superficiality; inattention to rudiments; undue time

The polite needlework of the parlour boarding school gave way to more useful sewing lessons—like this one at Streatham County Secondary School in 1913.

A classroom in Fulham County School in 1910. By this time girls' schools equalled boys' in serious teaching.

given to accomplishments, and those not taught intelligently or in any scientific manner; want of organisation—these may sufficiently indicate the character of the complaints we have received." Their report marked a turning point.

Miss Buss of the North London Collegiate School, and Miss Beale of Cheltenham Ladies' College were by this time well established enough to give evidence to the committee. But apart from their two schools, there were only a handful of institutions that have survived up to today. The Godolphin School in Salisbury and Casterton School (one of its early teachers was Charlotte Brontë) in Yorkshire were in existence, while in York there was a Quaker boarding school known as the Mount. The Mount had started up in 1821, and thus in 1894 it was able to produce a school song with a boast few schools could rival:

> There is a school of ancient fame
> All in the North countrie,
> Where thorough work and honest game
> Have long gone merrily.
>
> 'Tis here our Mothers used to be,
> And cousins not a few,
> And aunts and sisters formerly
> There did as now we do.

Shortly after the Commission's report, new girls' schools started springing up all over the place. Their pupils responded to the proper teaching with enthusiasm. "Perhaps most people would think it exaggerated if I said that, while I was in school, I lived in an almost constant state of bliss," wrote an early pupil of Notting Hill High

School. "But it would be true. I was ravenous for discipline, teaching, books, friends and leaders." In the same way Miss Constance Maynard, one of the early students of Hitchin, later to become Girton College, wrote, "The extraordinary happiness of that first year at Hitchin is a thing that cannot come twice in a lifetime . . ." This feeling of having been liberated from the dull routine of governess, and drawing room, accounts for much of the enthusiasm of the earlier songs.

Art, perhaps because it had once been a polite accomplishment, always seems to feature in early prospectuses–like this example from Caldecote Towers.

It was, therefore, in this spirit that the girls of St. Leonards would sing "St. Leonards for Aye", to the tune of "Hearts of Oak".

> Come, work well, my girls, 'tis at glory we aim,
> To add honours new to our 'lustrious name;
> Ever onward we're striving for Duty and Right,
> Our spirits are keen and our hearts free and light.
>
> *Chorus*
> "St. Leonards for aye" is our joyous refrain,
> We always are ready, steady, girls, steady,
> We'll work, and win honours again and again.

The new girls' schools sometimes experimented with gardening lessons. Putney County Secondary School put this picture in their prospectus.

To generations entirely accustomed to the idea of schools, it's difficult to remember the paralysing boredom of home life that must have been the alternative to institutions like St. Leonards. Equally well, we can hardly recapture the excitement of taking part in such a new venture. Edgbaston High School in Birmingham, which in 1976 celebrated its centenary, had a school song which explained something of this feeling.

> In Education's early days
> When High Schools there were none, sir,
> Some zealous pioneers there were
> And soon they started one, sir.
> All prejudice they did revoke,
> Set custom at a distance,
> The bonds of ignorance they broke
> And overcame resistance.
>
> *Chorus*
> And this as law we will maintain
> And this you must confess, sir,
> There is no school in all the land
> We love like E.H.S., sir.
>
> Miss Cooper as Head Mistress came,
> And founded our traditions;
> She showed the world what girls can do
> When stirred by high ambitions.
> For eighteen years she led us on
> With progress still increasing,
> And we will ever think of her
> With gratitude unceasing.

Headmistresses have often inspired gratitude among their pupils, and the first generation of proper school teachers did so more than most. They were genuinely remarkable women. The intrepid Miss Beale, for instance, learned to tricycle at the age of sixty-seven; she corresponded with Ruskin; and with Miss Buss spoke at innumerable meetings, cajoled, persuaded and sometimes bullied in the cause of girls' education. A little vignette of these two formidable women is preserved in an early and somewhat po-faced biography of Miss Beale. On a visit to an international conference about education, the two headmistresses wandered into a little restaurant near the Sorbonne, in Paris. "Miss Beale and Miss Buss found themselves in the midst of artists and students, some of whom carried on pronounced flirtations with the waitress girls. Miss Beale sat calmly writing her speech for the next meeting, indifferent to her déjeuner and unconscious of her surroundings," breathes her awed biographer.

No. 0127.—"Cheltenham" Dual Desk.

AS SUPPLIED TO THE LADIES' COLLEGE, CHELTENHAM

Made entirely of wood. Desk and Standards made of **Best Pitch Pine**, Chair Seats and Backs of Beech. Locker with hinged Top for each pupil, Dovetailed Corners, Footrail. Very suitable for Ladies' Schools, the separate Chair Seats and Backs being specially conducive to comfort while working. Length, 3 feet 6 inches; width of top, 18½ inches; seat, 15 inches.

Heights, 32 inches and 30 inches; Floor Space, 42 inches.

Can be made any height.

Price, including *Staining and Varnishing* ... ... per Desk, 33s. 0d.
Also made with sliding top, thus allowing the Seats and Desk to be nearer than usual when the Pupils are sitting. Price, including *Staining and Varnishing* ... per Desk, 37s. 6d.

The influence of Miss Beale and Cheltenham Ladies' College could even sell school desks, as the Educational Supply Association's catalogue of 1912 reveals.

The Queen Elizabeth's Grammar School for Girls in Barnet had a song which contrasts past days with present.

> Sing we the song of days gone by,
> Of those who strove 'mid dust and heat
> The lighted heart and mind to bring
> To hall or crowded street.
> No outpost of an alien band,
> They gazed afar from this fair height,
> Pledged to the conquest greater far
> Of ignorance and night.
>
> Sing we the song of days that are
> When in this School these dreams come true,
> When science in her power reveals
> This old world ever new;
> When tongues of other lands we learn
> And know all men our brothers be;
> Whilst thro' the past we learn to trace
> Some purpose of Eternity.

Naturally the pioneers had enormous influence, not just over the form of a school (Miss Buss's North London was frequently visited by would-be school founders to see how it worked), but also over the curriculum. A generation later a Board of Education report summed up the changes that had been going on since the 1864 report. "St. Leonards and boarding schools of a similar type in England, while retaining the ordinary subjects of study in girls' schools, have also adopted other subjects from the boys' curriculum, as well as the whole public-school plan..." What they had *not* borrowed, however, was the wholesale concentration on the classics. Miss Beale was none too keen on the classics—at least, when they were studied from an early age. "I feel strongly that Latin should, however, properly come after German specially for girls," she wrote in her influential book, *Work and Play in Girls' Schools*. "There is a pestilential atmosphere in the Campania and one needs to have one's moral fibre braced by the poetry of the Hebrews, and of England and Germany, if one would remain unaffected by writings saturated with heathen thought." On more practical grounds a contributor to her book pointed out, "Girls' schools have grown up with other traditions; music and drawing and modern languages have so long been the staple of a girl's education that it is perhaps too late now to make any radical change."

Dancing was a tradition of girls' education that the new public and high schools took over from the parlour boarding schools. But generations of tall girls have, unfortunately, learned only the man's rôle as girl had to dance with girl. The girls at Fulham County School in 1910 face the same problem.

Latin girls' school songs are therefore comparatively rare—though there are dozens of Latin songs in boys' schools. The Haberdashers' Aske's School for Girls used to sing one which began:

> Mater nostra quae securas
> Servas aede filias
> Cuius stabilis virtute
> Vivimus communitas
> Tu perennis, nos diurnae,
> Parvis clausum terminis
> Spatium juventutis, schola
> Restat perdurabilis.

Translated, this means "Our mother, you who keep safe and sound your daughters in your house, by whose virtue we live as a firmly fixed community, you last for ever, we are fleeting, the period of youth is closed within a short compass, the school remains for ever."

Another full-length Latin song I have come across is one still sung by the Orme Girls' School, a voluntary-aided grammar school whose governors in 1977 were seeking independence. Orme girls still sung their song, which was stuck into the hymnbooks. "The song when sung by all 600-odd female voices can bring excitement to the heart," a pupil told me. "A very much modernised and jazzed up version of the song is sung by many of us when there are no teachers about. (Sometimes fooling about and adding Yeh, Yeh, Yeh on the end of each line can be very effective!)" Written by a classics mistress, Miss H. M. Barnard, in the 1920s, its first verse praises earlier generations.

> Nunc canenedum, nunc laetandum,
> Illos nunc laudemus
> Qui dederunt conservanda
> Haec quibus gaudemus:
> Bonos omnes fundatores
> Gratae efferamus:
> Quae dederunt conservando
> Semper floreamus.

This means in English. "It is right for us, of the present generation, to sing in joy as we praise the people who have given to us for the rest of our lives the opportunities which we enjoy. May we pay respect to all our generous founders and be grateful to them; by using their gifts, may we grow in wisdom always."

More common is the occasional Latin motto. Esdaile, a fee-paying school in Edinburgh, had this Latin end to every English verse:

> Floreant caritas, pietas, veritas,
> Floreat semper Collegium!

"New girls, too young to know any Latin, were always teased by being told the chorus meant: Flowers, carrots, peas and vegetables all flourish in the school garden," comments Mrs. Judith Caulfield, an old girl. The words were by J. M. Caie, a father of one of the pupils. The school was an early foundation of 1863 to help to educate daughters of ministers of the Church of Scotland.

In those high days of Empire, there was the confident assumption that the glory that was Greece and the grandeur that was Rome had been superseded by the British red on the map. Civilisation, as we knew it, was firmly administered overseas by British men and women, and it followed that its cradle was the British schools. Older-shaw School for Girls, Merseyside, had a song which expressed this:

The stream of Man's life rose in mist-covered mountains,
His strength ebbs and springs as a tide flowing high,
Babylonia and Egypt are lost in the sandhills,
The glory of England stands bright 'gainst the sky.
We seek for the law of its righteous abiding,
We strive for the truth which will make all men free,
With disciplined fervour we seek her up-building
Man's City of God won by toil from the sea.

The line about "disciplined fervour" seems to echo Miss Beale's feelings about the less wholesome fervours of the Campania. At St. Michael's Hall, Hove, the idea that girls' schools cradled the new civilisation was made more explicit. Happy days, when schoolgirls could sing with confidence:

What need to seek from Greece or Rome
A subject for our song,
While still there stands so near at home
The place where we belong?
What theme could poet more rejoice,
What more befit our lays,
Than that in which we lift our voice
To sing St. Michael's praise?

'Tis here that Knowledge plays her part
Our budding minds to train;
For maths and history, science, art,
Build up a healthy brain.
So Memory grows unafraid,
And Thought begins to play,
While Fancy lends its magic aid
And Reason holds its sway.

In their search for a proper education, it was mathematics which seemed, to the early headmistresses, to hold the key. Geometry, then mainly consisting of Euclid's propositions, aroused Miss Beale's passions. "To study geometry is to enter a new path, and we do not see at first to what heights it leads, upwards to the universe of ideas." Something about the idea of girlhood learning Euclid's propositions seems to have stirred the Victorian mind. Could maths and true womanliness be compatible? A member of the 1864 Commission had had this to say: "It happens that the finest manners I ever saw among young people—the most perfect self-possession, modesty and freedom from affection—were in a class of girls who were brought to me to demonstrate a proposition in Euclid."

Euclid's propositions were a series of geometrical definitions which in theory had to be proved'. In practice, they could be learned by heart. An early pupil of the Skinners' Company School for Girls, Stamford Hill, remembers the confusion when Euclid suddenly became geometry. "The order of the propositions had mysteriously changed; we were expected to do things with protractor and compasses, and generally to exhibit a non-existent mathematical intelligence." Despite this early disappearance of Euclid (most schools seem to have dropped him around 1900) I have discovered one school song which used to hymn his glories. Again, it is the same happy optimism—Euclid and other serious studies make us the inheritors and surpassers of ancient civilisations. The girls of the City of Bath's Girls' School, now part of Hayesfield Comprehensive, used to sing:

> Sing now and take the song
> Stone streets and hills along
> Kindling endeavour:
> Knowing our city's fame,
> Great since the Romans came,
> Raise and renew her name
> Gracious for ever.
>
> Keen in the work we find,
> Honest and clear in mind,
> Bunsen flames burning;
> Old tales or Euclid's show,
> Homecraft or things that grow,
> Rocks and the winds that blow
> Follow with learning.

"Bunsen flames burning": the girls of Fulham County School cultivate a healthy brain in 1910.

The second verse had to be dropped when Euclid disappeared. Science and Bunsen burners, however, remained awesome topics. At Thoresby High School, the song had a charming North of England pride:

Where learning sits with glory crowned, we strive to enter in,
Though science rolls her vapours round and frights us with her din.
Let history pelt us with her dates and language growl in scorn,
We know that we shall force her gates, for we are Yorkshire born.

As they struggled to compete on equal terms with boys, examinations were a source of even more fear and worry to the early pupils than they are now. Opinion was divided as to their use. Emily Davies, who founded Girton, and Frances Mary Buss were insistent that girls must take the same examinations as boys. Anne Jemima Clough of Newnham and Dorothea Beale felt that since the examinations system for boys needed reforming anyway, it might be better to have a specially adapted system for girls. There was much in their favour, but Emily Davies voiced the fears of her lobby when she explained: "We do not want certificates of proficiency given to half-educated women. There are examinations which will do this already within reach." In the end examinations, on the same system as those in boys' schools, became widely accepted. The result was a crop of examination songs. Kingsley School, Horley, which originally was sited in North London, took a tune ("If you're anxious for to shine") from *Patience*, the Gilbert and Sullivan opera, for one of their exam songs.

Do not walk into your class feeling sure you will not pass,
But go in and do your best,
For you very soon will find that some thoughts will fill your mind,
And your pen will do the rest;
Do not fear to make mistakes in names of towns or history dates,
But make a valiant shot,
For 'tis better to have tried than to cast it all aside,
Whether it is right or not.

Chorus
And everyone will say,
When reports come home one day;
Whether she was first or last or not, she has tried quite hard we see;
Well, what a very conscientious type of girl,
The Kingsley girl must be.

There's also a particularly jolly "Matriculation Success song", to inspire those faint hearts facing the dreaded matriculation exams. (For those too young to remember matric, it was a system of amassing credits in what would now be known as school certificate, or O-level exams. Various subjects, such as maths, were compulsory.) Kingsley School is now no more, and I have not been able to discover on what occasions this exam song was sung—whether before to cheer the spirits, or after to celebrate.

> When they sat in the hot stuffy room,
> And looked through the papers so dull,
> Their spirits at zero, no longer a hero,
> They fancied great honours to cull;
> But in spite of their gloomy despair,
> They shone so with brilliance and wit,
> That the School now acclaims them, and the Varsity owns them,
> With full right of entry to it.

There was no greater success. Oxford or Cambridge was the aim of the girls who came from schools founded by Old Girtonians. Thus, at Wycombe Abbey, they sang:

> Soon we are Seniors and past is our playtime,
> Oxford and Cambridge, the world or the home
> Claim our devotion, so now in our Maytime
> Cheer we our School ere we start forth to roam.

Those never-to-be-forgotten Honours Boards adorn nearly every older school with names now meaning nothing, yet something to look at for the young pupils during a boring Speech Day and something more to the aspiring university student.

> Here in our Hall, where our records of glory,
> Blaze from the boards in the gold-lettered names . . .

went one of the St. Leonards songs.

The message of many school songs was that hard work would achieve wonders—if failure occurs, just try again. The battle for honours was the subject of the second verse of the Portsmouth High School, a GPDST foundation.

> When term work is hard and exams are before us,
> When for prizes and honours we labour in vain,
> Undaunted by failure, let this re-assure us,
> They fight best who beaten will fight on again.
> In all our keen struggles at desk or at wicket,
> At work with our forms, or at play at the courts,
> When we glory in tennis, or hockey, or cricket,
> It is fair play that wins both at lessons and sports.

In a less exalted vein, but with the same underlying idea, the girls of Haverstock Central School in North London, took the view:

Fair play at cricket at Caldecote Towers about the time of the First World War.

> Now maths and French and history
> Make idle scholars sad,
> And grammar and geography
> Are apt to be as bad,
> But we are wise and always try
> To tackle them with "vim";
> To shirk and grumble only makes our
> Schooldays rather grim.
> Haverstock, Haverstock, cloudy days or fine,
> Haverstock, Haverstock, every day a line.
> The school we do our best in,
> And learn to work and rest in,
> And play the game with zest in,
> Haverstock for aye.

The idea that even tedious tasks must be done with strenuous energy is another idea that's out of fashion. If learning becomes only easy pleasure and the drudgery has been taken out of it, then we are far, indeed, from the world of our foremothers.

Playing the game with zest—an early illustration of hockey in the 1890s. So keen is the struggle that some are even losing their hats.

Miss Beale didn't believe in examinations, nor did she believe in the spur of competition ("Public prize-givings seem to me very undesirable"), but she did believe in effort. Peterborough County Grammar School for Girls agreed:

> Is it work? Then strive our utmost;
> Honest labour answers all.
> Wealth of knowledge spread before us,
> Let us listen to its call.
> Quick, alert to help each other
> For the glory of the School
> And obey with cheerful promptness
> Every wise and honoured rule.

It followed that "doing your best" was what really mattered, and several school songs consoled the unscholastic.

> We can't all be athletes, we can't all be clever,
> But there's one thing that oldest and youngest may share—
> To strive for Beaumanor, to do our best ever,
> To strive for Beaumanor whose proud name we bear

sang the girls of Beaumanor House, of the Newarthe Girls' School, Leicester. In much the same way, the Hull High School for Girls pointed out that not everybody could succeed.

Students we of learning's pages,
Writ through centuries of time;
Fact and figure, song and story,
Woven into form sublime,
Though of olive, bay or laurel,
Tribute none on brow be set . . .
Though not ev'ry one among us,
Wears successes' coronet:

Chorus
Three crowns we may rightly covet,
Crown of work in youth begun,
Crown of brave, untiring effort,
Crown of duty nobly done.

Effort . . . duty . . . the very words are now expected to raise a smile.
And yet what could be more inspiring than Miss Beale's dictum on
the subject, "We cannot make it too clear that good may be better
than best, and that the only praise we should desire to hear is 'She
hath done what she could'."?

Playing the Game

4

"Hockey is certainly nothing if not progressive," wrote Miss E. M. Robson, secretary of the All England Women's Hockey Association in 1889. She was being quite serious. Hockey was very much the new thing in those days—thought by some to be "fast", and certainly daring, if not naughty. In the same way that the new serious education produced songs praising study, so the gloriously untrammelled freedom of the playing fields gave rise to school songs.

Previously, exercise in a Victorian girls' boarding school would have been merely a matter of "taking a turn" round the garden, or perhaps going for a walk outside the grounds in charge of a mistress. At expensive schools, riding (sidesaddle, of course) was sometimes on the curriculum. Otherwise the most in the way of physical education would have been calisthenic exercises, a sort of gentle P.T. These exercises were often combined with truly fiercesome gadgets called backboards, wooden boards bound upon the back, designed to correct usually imaginary curvatures of the spine. Worse still, in the interests of good posture, wretched girls were sometimes made to promenade up and down stairs wearing, not a book on the head, but something called an "Iron Crown". "Conceive the injury which must arise to the brain of anyone, especially that of a growing girl, by the imposition of *a weight which averages fifty lbs.*" wrote a gymnastics expert.

a   *b*

Calisthenics became a little more energetic, and the new high schools sometimes took it up in the form of "drill". At Croydon High School for Girls drilling was taken by Sergeant-Major Burke and consisted largely of simple arm exercises and a lot of marching.

The gentle nature of drilling is obvious from a drill song written by Miss Medina Griffiths of Caldecote Towers. Drill Song No. 1 was distinctly feminine, and sounds not at all energetic by today's standards.

> Swinging, swinging, onward we go,
> Rising, falling, gently and low.
> Turning, bending, marching along,
> Singing, singing, sweetly our song.

An early drill lesson at Shrewsbury High School, a Girls' Public Day School Trust foundation.

below: Gymnastic exercises with "Swing and Stirrups" appliance.

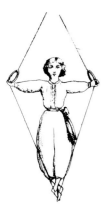

Drilling remained in girls' schools right up to the last war, and Sports Days were often enlivened by the sight of scores of girls marching in formation. The Royal Victoria Patriotic School, an establishment for orphaned daughters of soldiers of the Crimean War and one which seems to have applied almost military discipline to girls, had this particularly rousing marching song:

> Attention, ye worthy citizens, and hold your heads up high,
> For the Children of the Forces, we now are passing by.
> Inheritors of honour from land and sky and sea,
> Now harken to the war cry of these Men of Pedigree.
> Roy, roy, royally we'll muster and we'll fight
> For the vic, vic, victory that always follows Right,
> For the pat, pat, patriotic nation we will be,
> For the honour of our country and the R.V.P.

By about the 1870s not only drill, but also more energetic gymnastic exercises were beginning to be accepted. Madame Brenner, who kept a gymnasium in Bruton Street, off Berkeley Square, wrote *Gymnastics for Ladies* in 1870 and concluded: "I earnestly trust I have satisfied those to whom I have spoken through this volume, that Gymnastics Practice, carried out by the Educated, and in the spirit of refinement and conscientiousness, can never be objectionable to the feelings and habits of the True Lady."

Hoop exercise in Madame Brenner's gymnasium. "Marching not only promotes an equality of carriage," she wrote, "but contributes to a general orderly manner and conduct between certain intervals of the Gymnastic Practice. But Marching is rather dull work for Ladies: and therefore I direct it to be performed in different gradations of time while trundling the Hoop."

A decade later, the real breakthrough came with the advent of hockey. In 1887 the first private hockey club was started and only seven years later after "an informal preliminary meeting at a teashop in Brighton" the All England Women's Hockey Association had been formed. It spread like wildfire. By the end of the century hockey was the "chief winter game at Oxford and Cambridge Ladies' Colleges and at schools which make a speciality of physical exercise such as Wimbledon House School (now Roedean School, Brighton) and St. Leonards School".

The girls of the pioneering St. Leonards, founded in 1877, were able, a decade later, to sing with vigour:

> There ne'er was a school which with ours could compete,
> Throughout Britain's realm ne'er its equal we meet;
> For not only our minds but our bodies we train,
> And we work with a will and we play might and main.
>
> 'Tis stated by some that too much we essay,
> That girls ought to have milder sports for their play,
> But our health and our actions that statement belie;
> So "Hurrah for our School and our Head" is our cry.

At the other games-pioneering establishment, Wimbledon House (later Roedean), a song grandly titled "Wimbledonia" mentioned the delights of the playing field.

> Hockey triumphs all are thine,
> All thy freaks are liberty,
> Wimbledonia, blithe and merry,
> Lasting health I wish to thee.
>
> *Chorus*
> Wimbledonia, fair and free,
> Health and strength belong to thee,
> Felix Wimbledonia.

Hockey triumphs in 1910 during the Hertfordshire Ladies' Hockey Tournament. Note the long skirts and ties.

For any normal girl of the 1890s, hockey was irresistible. Hockey literally meant freedom—freedom from stays. 'By far the most formidable barrier in the way of easy, graceful and efficient play is the deplorable practice of wearing tight corsets," wrote Mr. Leonard Williams, M.B., in the Isthmian Library book on the game. "In the hockey field (except perhaps those known as riding stays), they are nothing short of an abomination."

Nor was freedom from stays the only advantage. Skirts were excitingly *short*. *"The skirt*, as commonly worn, is too long. At the most it should reach no further than midway between the knee and ankle," wrote Mr. Williams. "A long skirt not only impedes running, but it leads to practices, such as curtsying to stop the ball, which are very ungraceful and are certainly not hockey." Nor was curtsying the only ungraceful trick practised by unscrupulous lady players. Some would all but catch the ball by planting their feet apart, bending their knees and straining the skirt across them. The Isthmian Library volume illustrated these disgraceful tactics with the comment, "Figs. 49 and 50 show simple ways of stopping the ball, without losing it, by an *indefensible* use of the skirt."

The "indefensible use of the skirt," either by curtseying (left) or by planting legs apart (right), in order to stop the ball in its folds.

No wonder, then, that the keen hockey players of Westfield College paid tribute to the hockey skirt with a song to be sung to the "Tarpaulin Jacket".

> A stalwart young forward sat sighing,
> And as o'er corrections she pored, she pored,
> Her thoughts kept a flitting and flying,
> As she thought of the goals she once scored.
>
> *Chorus*
> Oh, give me my pads and my bulger,
> And give me my short hockey skirt,
> And find me ten merry young comrades
> Who don't mind the wind, rain or dirt.
>
> Oh, the glories of battling with Bedford,
> Tho' friendly with them at the last,
> And the glories of conquering a crisis,
> Are now become things of the past.

A bulger was a poetic name for a hockey stick, not (as I myself first thought) a protective undergarment. But protective garments were worn. "All players should wear shin-guards—they prevent injury and give confidence." For not the least advantage of the game was that it was positively bloodthirsty. In an age when young ladies were meant to be feminine and deportment and propriety were the norm, to be tearing up and down a pitch, shouting with excitement, hacking away at a ball, covered in mud, was bliss.

Girton produced in 1894 a particularly militant song, commemorating hockey-pitch rivalry with its fellow Cambridge College, Newnham. Sung to the tune of "Wot Cher", it goes:

> To our ground there came a hostile force;
> They were bent on beating us, of course;
> And the College cheered till it grew hoarse,
> While fiercer still and fiercer grew the fray.
> See our players in their scarlet shirts,
> Tassel'd hockey caps and short blue skirts;
> Little reck they of their wounds and hurts—
> These are all the order of the day.
>
> *Chorus*
> "Play up!" all the College cried;
> "Pass out to the wing, girls!
> "That's the sort of thing, girls!"
> Run! I thought I should have died!
> Knocked it through the Newnham goal!

I've no patience with those whiny folk,
Who when both their legs are nearly broke,
Will not treat the matter as a joke,
Take things as they come and show some pluck.
Here's to all who play a sturdy game,
On the Hockey Ground, their field of fame,
To the glory of the College name;
Here's to all the team and their good luck!

And after the match, the mud and the bruises, came the glorious hot bath. Westfield College celebrated this moment:

And when at last the game is o'er, they turn their steps to College,
And tho' with shins and ankles sore and bruises passing knowledge,
Their merry song rings loud and clear as in their baths they steam-O,
Those most surprising, early rising, enterprising, Amazons,
The Westfield College team-O.

An early verse of the same song makes it clear that a lot of fun could be had out of hockey clothes. The puritanical Mr. Williams might declare, "There must be . . . no offerings to the Belial of the fashion-plate or the Molock of impressionable spectators; for the time being the player is no longer a lady, whose social position is suitably expressed in her attire, she is a workwoman . . ." Hockey players were quite conscious of the impressionable spectators; and colours and style were all important. Girtonians wore blue skirts, scarlet shirts and tasselled hockey caps, while Westfield had snazzy blue and red and white:

The "workwoman" player in full form. 1913 hockey pioneer Miss Balfour of the Hertfordshire Ladies' team takes a penalty corner.

> In hockey matches of today, when there is any fighting,
> The Westfield team goes forth to play, to watch is most exciting,
> In tunics blue and girdles red, and blouses white and cream-O,
> These most athletic, unaesthetic, energetic warriors,
> The Westfield hockey team-O.

The rationale of the games field was, of course, that it promoted physical health. "Games of all kinds are so much more valuable than mere walking," wrote Miss Frances Dove of Wycombe Abbey, "because walking is so purely mechanical... In them is always a special interest upon which the mind must be concentrated, and which therefore entirely prevents the possibility of the thoughts dwelling upon the subject of the last lesson."

But games became more than just recreation. They became nearly an obsession, with almost every school which had a songbook possessing also a hockey song. Even the Quakers' Mount had their hockey song, though their game was originally played to somewhat odd rules, which allowed any number on the field.

> Oh, you must come to hockey today,
> For it matters not how many play,
> Let us follow the ball—for the best game of all
> Is the game that we're playing today.

While at Queen Elizabeth's Grammar School for Girls in Mansfield, Nottinghamshire, the hockey song, sung by the whole school after victory, was loyal to the last girl.

> Oh hockey, hockey players, you are good 'uns heart and hand;
> You're a credit to your calling and to all your loyal band,
> May your wind be never failing, may your shots be ever true;
> Hurrah! ye hockey players, here's success to all of you.

It wasn't just hockey, of course, that stirred the schoolgirl soul. The course of the seasons brought round different games. Just as the Paris sophisticate can chart the time of year by the Spring or Autumn collections, so eager schoolgirls noted the passing of time by the game they were playing. The Whitchurch High School song had a charming verse:

> Sturdy of limb and quick of eye
> The hockey runners go,
> When keen across the playing fields
> The wintry breezes blow;
> But when the smiling summer sun
> Looks down from azure skies,
> The straight ball skimming o'er the net
> Like winged light'ning flies!

"The straight ball skimming o'er the net"–tennis at Putney County Secondary School for Girls in about 1918.

In a more elaborate form, the same idea is conveyed by a Wycombe Abbey song, written in 1902. (Wycombe, it should be remembered, was a particularly sporting school and its founder, Miss Dove, a keen believer in physical education.)

When the holidays are over, and the term is well begun,
When our lesson books are put away, and the morning's work is done,
Then we rush forth from the boot room, before the clock strikes two,
For all of us are very keen to play lacrosse anew.

Chorus
Pass, catch, pass again. Keep it in the air.
Now the Centre's caught it, so down the field we tear.

Now the hockey season follows, and our sticks are routed out,
When we've bullied at the centre, we begin to slash about.
We're fighting for our honour, for we want to win the cup,
And the lusty shouts around us bid us not to give it up.

Chorus
HIC, HAC, HOC away, set it on the roll.
Pass it down to somebody and quickly shoot a goal.

But the summer term is best, for we are out from morn to night,
Then we run out to play cricket as soon as it is light.
And we lie beneath the beeches when the sun is overhead,
Then cricket in the evening till it's time to go to bed.

Chorus
Slog, run, run again, you're running up the score.
Now do look out for catches. How's that for leg before?

Cricket was a particularly popular game, and like hockey was played with enthusiasm made greater because it too required a certain freedom of dress. "Above all," remarked Lady Milner, expert cricket contributor to the *Gentlewoman's Book of Sports,* "let us not spoil our freedom of movement by encasing ourselves in steel armour, more commonly called 'the correct corset'; though this word I mention with bated breath, and with a humble apology for any masculine reader whose eye may happen to stray over these pages . . . In your pursuit of a ball, let there not be ominous creakings of whalebone and splitting of side seams to delay your onward flight." Hats, however, were *de rigueur*.

Roedean had a special song for the First Eleven with this heroine-worshipping chorus:

Oh! the Cricket First Eleven,
We admire on every hand,
'Tis the one above all others,
We love best in all the land.
May your scores be never failing,
And your bowling ever true!
Oh! noble First Eleven,
Here's the best of healths to you.

An early cricket match in 1922. Cricket pioneer Lady Milner had this reassuring comment about girls' behaviour on the field: "If the anxious parent is a little afraid of her daughter indulging in the dangerous pastime of flirtation, she can have no better protection than the other twenty-one ladies and the isolation of her position in the field required by the rules of cricket!"

The excitement of the match is best conveyed by a Kingsley School cricket song, which goes right through the course of a match. For those not expert in cricket technology I will spare them the whole song. Kingsley doesn't open the batting but by the fourth verse their men are at the stumps.

> Full pitchers, breaks or even sneaks
> Approach, while batsmen are sighing;
> But Kingsley's eye is ever straight
> For balls go flying, flying.
> The score mounts up in twos and threes
> And fours, Umpires are meeting;
> So fielders fast must play if they
> Would Kingsley team be beating.

Such was Kingsley School's fondness for song, that their songbook commemorates not only hockey, cricket and netball, but also ping-pong and tennis:

> Athletic Kingsley! Athletic Kingsley!
> You've the girls to keep the School its tennis name;
> Whether they're beaten or whether they've conquered,
> They leave the courts with smiling faces just the same.

Similar sportswomanship is celebrated by the netball song of Queen Elizabeth's Grammar School, Mansfield, written by Miss E. Marchant.

> Oh, the netball team is a stalwart band,
> They are seven good men and true;
> For they pass the ball from hand to hand,
> And the shooter puts it through—
> Oh! the shooter puts it through.
>
> Though they sometimes win and they sometimes lose,
> Still they always play the game;
> And that's what we'd have if we could but choose,
> So let's cheer them all the same—
> Oh! let's cheer them all the same.

A stalwart band of netball players at Southwark Park Secondary School in 1912.

At Bedford College, there was even a boating song:

> Then row, Stroke, row, put your strength to the oar,
> Follow her Bow, never look to the shore,
> Now both together; one great stroke more
> For the College, Fame and Glory.

So seductive was the lure of the playing field that at St. Margaret's School, Bushey, there grew up an elaborate ritual known as The Games Tea. After a staff-versus-girls cricket or rounders match at the end of the summer term, came this remarkable event. Team members, senior and leaving girls each escorted in a member of staff to the dining room. Indeed, they *skipped* in, arm-in-arm, according to old girls Pamela Cleaver and Penny Cudmore who have recalled the ritual for the present old girls' magazine. Perhaps the most unusual thing of all was the way different teams wore different flowers. There were laurels for the first tennis team, sweet peas for the cricketers with rhubarb leaves for the scorers, cow parsley for the first netball team and cornflowers for the second. The school fire brigade wore marigolds and fireweed. The headgirl was in charge, and the junior IV form washed up! During tea, the smallest girl in the school rang a bell, then asked the headgirl to announce the Odes. These were specially written for the occasion, dedicated to different sports, usually recalling the year's triumphs or setbacks. Finally the whole school rose to its feet and sang The Games Tea Song, which started off:

> We've played our games together
> In every kind of weather,
> And now we meet to celebrate
> With pomp and revelry,
> The health of all the games we love
> We've played with mirth and glee.

A completely different, and more than a little unsporting, ritual was developed by Walthamstowe High School. The school adopted a kind of war cry, which was relentlessly chanted during matches with opposing schools. Bellowed by girlish voices, it went like this:

> Boom! Boom! Boom! Chick-a-boom!
> Boom ricka ticka ticka boom!
> Boom, catch a rat trap
> Bigger than a cat trap,
> Boom! Boom! Boom!
> Cannibal, cannibal, sis boom bah!
> Walthamstowe High School—Yah, Yah, Yah!

It is little wonder games came to play such a large part in schoolgirl life (and indeed schoolgirl fiction). The expectations of the early games pioneers were large. "I think I do not speak too strongly when I say that games," wrote Miss Dove, "i.e. active games in the open air, are essential to a healthy existence and that most of the qualities, if not all, that conduce to the supremacy of our country in so many quarters of the globe, are fostered, if not solely developed, by means of games." She went on to claim, "Games have a much higher function to perform in school life than any I have yet mentioned. Here is a splendid field for the development of powers of organisation, of good temper under trying circumstances, courage and determination to play up and do your best even in a losing game, rapidity of thought and action, judgment and self-reliance, and, above all things, unselfishness, and a knowledge of corporate action, learning to sink individual preferences in the effort of loyally working with others for the common good."

Sinking individual preferences in a game of lacrosse at Roedean in 1962. Lacrosse was a game imported to Britain from America. One reason why it may have caught on is that the key skill is "cradling"– i.e. keeping the ball in the net by a rocking motion.

The highest compliment that could be paid after a hard cricket match was: "Your girls play like gentlemen and behave like ladies." The ethos of the sports field began to take on that peculiarly British stiff upper lip. It's reflected in this games song from Belvedere School, the GPDST school in Liverpool.

Oh it's fine to belong to Belvedere,
With a name to defend and a past to revere,
To be given the right to swell the cheer
For a team on a tournament morning.

We are proud of our teams as they take the field;
We are proud of their struggle, though they lose the shield,
Be it raquet or crosse that with honour they wield,
In a match on the tournament morning.

Chorus
With respect and honour we will treat our foe,
Whate'er our emotion, it shall not show.
For their lives they can't tell if we win or no
By our mien on the tournament morning.

The idea of playing the game, team spirit, esprit de corps and so forth spread like wildfire. There is hardly a school song that doesn't have at least one glancing reference to the virtues of the playing fields. Folkestone County School for Girls, now the Folkestone Grammar School for Girls, had a fine song, among the verses of which was this:

With joyous zest run forth to play the game,
Let fusty sluggishness be put to shame.
The dazzling whiteness of wise truth revere,
And rainbow lights of beauty shining clear.

Learning to play the game at Saison School for Girls in 1958. The lesson for the day was "first steps in ball control".

At Glasgow High School, now Cleveden Secondary School, the song had a verse which went:

> Not all with high distinctions bring
> New lustre to thy name,
> But all are privileged to sing,
> "We learn to play the game."

Some songs went much further. In Salford, the London Street School for Girls had a song with almost every line about the ethics of games.

> Whatsoever in this life you have to do,
> Play the game,
> Win and laugh but learn to lose and laugh as well,
> Play the game
> They are fools who bounce and brag.
> You must fight, don't mind the fag.
> Solid grit's the stuff that's always bound to tell.
> Play the game.
>
> *Chorus*
> Play the game, play the game,
> All true Britons do the same.
> Win the goal by honest work.
> Never sham and never shirk.
> Play the game, play the game, play the game.

The school's formidable headmistress, Miss Gornall, had a favourite saying for Sports Day, recalled for me by Mrs. A. L. Cheetham. "Remember, girls," she would say, "to win gives prestige to our school: to lose with grace adds character, making the two efforts equal."

After the match, the mud, and the bruises there is the glorious prospect of the hot bath. Lacrosse players on their way back to Roedean in 1951.

It is at St. Paul's Girls' School, Hammersmith, however, that the last word in the games field ethic comes. In 1912, when Gustav Holst was teaching the St. Paulinas music, the "Playground Song" was produced. The author was probably Miss Constance Flood-Jones, the art mistress—though earlier a competition had been held among the pupils for a suitable song. The version that Miss Flood-Jones produced has everything—the joy in games, its usefulness in teaching the team spirit, and—important point—its usefulness in life outside school.

> With joyful hearts our song we raise
> For many a jocund scene.
> In swimming bath, gymnasium
> And playground cool and green.
> 'Tis there we learn to do our work
> With all our might and main,
> The rules to keep in friendly strife
> For naught but Honour's gain.
>
> *Chorus*
> So when with other schools we vie
> We'll fear no lasting shame.
> "Come Victory or Failure,
> St. Paul's will play the game."
>
> When forth to wider fields we go
> In Life's great game to play,
> That self-control and vigilance
> That we have learned today
> Shall rule us still and keep our choice
> Obedient to the Right,
> Shall work with us and weigh with us
> And help us in the fight.
>
> *Chorus*
> What e'er the future that we meet
> Our cry shall be the same,
> "Come Victory or Failure
> St. Paul's will play the game."

Mottoes, Flowers and Colours

5

Once the overwhelmingly important questions of work and sports had been organised, the newly-founded girls' high schools and public schools turned their attention to that rather nebulous subject, school tradition. With touching enthusiasm they adorned themselves with all the trappings—school song, coats of arms, badges, mottoes and school colours. The boys' schools had them: nothing less would do for girls. "School tradition is an impalpable thing," wrote Miss Sara Burstall, headmistress of Manchester High School in 1907. "The building and the ritual of daily life are its body; such things as labels on the books, the time-honoured fashions of moving through the passages and up the staircase, the names of bits of technique peculiar to the place. School colours and badges symbolise it; school songs give it utterance, and echo in the memory when school days are over."

A romantic unicorn badge and inspiring motto from James Gillespie's High School.

It is difficult for a present-day schoolgirl to see the importance of all this, or to imagine the days when the choice of a motto was of great importance. At the Skinners' Company School for Girls, Stamford Hill, the proposed mottoes were voted on. "The subsequent voting showed a large majority in favour of 'Honour before Honours'." What high-minded days those were, and the memory lingers on in the mottoes still to be found in the *Girls' Public School Yearbook*, "Trouthe and Honour, Freedom and Curteisie" (Park School, Glasgow), "Quietness and Strength" (Queen Anne's, Reading), "In fide vade" (Wycombe Abbey), "Pro Ecclesia Dei" (Old Palace School). "We wield ourselves as a weapon is wielded" was the motto of Peckham Secondary School, displayed on a long scroll at the back wall of the school hall. Tamworth High School in the Midlands had "With Goodwill doing Service" illuminated and framed above one pane of the gymnasium's double doors. On the other side was this stirring quotation from Tennyson's *The Princess*.

> O lift your natures up;
> Embrace our aims: work out your freedom. Girls,
> Knowledge is now no more a fountain seal'd,
> Drink deep until the habits of the slave,
> The sins of emptiness, gossip and spite
> And slander, die. Better not to be at all
> Than not be noble.

Militant mottoes contributed to many a stirring school song. Mrs. Ethel Walton, who ran a private school, Queen's School in Margate, chose the motto "Quaerite Summa", or "Strive for the highest". Possibly it had originated with her father, a headmaster who had brought up his daughter in boys' schools, to play cricket and other games. The song she wrote to go with the motto is refreshingly fiery.

> Our fathers brave in days of yore
> With valour bold went forth to war,
> Went forth to conquer or to die,
> And proudly raised their battle cry.
> Like them our battle cry we raise
> As we encounter life's rough ways,
> God and our duty is our call,
> Thus best for each thus best for all.
> Strive for the highest, our motto bold
> Strive with the might of our fathers of old,
> Quaerite Summa. Proclaim it on high.
> Quaerite Summa. Our school's battle cry.

At its rousing best, a school motto could produce a very creditable shout to cheer on the school team. At Harrogate College, where the motto was "Per Ardua ad Alta" (Through straits to heights), one of the school songs, written by Miss M. L. Davies, was bawled out at lacrosse matches. Its chorus, in particular, could strike fear into the breast of visiting teams.

Queen's School, Margate

List of Clothes Required for
WINTER TERMS

SCHOOLWEAR.

1 Dark green Gaberdine tunic.
1 School Hat.
1 Green Overall (Seniors).
2 Green Overalls (under 12).
1 Light frock (for dancing).
1 Uniform sports kilt, sweater, cap and scarf.

1 Green mackintosh.
1 Dark green overcoat (no fur).
1 Girdle.
2 Pairs tan gloves.

SUNDAYS.

1 Dark green frock.
1 Best hat with band.

UNDERCLOTHING.

3 Sets.
2 Pairs woven white knickers.
2 Pairs black silk hose (Seniors).

3 Pairs woven green knickers.
4 Pairs black cashmere hose or ¾ socks (under 12).
1 Dressing gown.

FOOTWEAR

2 Pairs black walking shoes.
1 Pair black house shoes (rubber or quarter rubber heels, not high).
1 Pair Lacrosse boots (Easter term).

1 Pair black gym shoes.
1 Pair bedroom slippers.
1 Pair hockey shoes (with bars) (Christmas term).
1 Pair Hockey pads (Christmas term).

SUNDRIES

3 Sheets.
3 Pillow Slips.
3 Serviettes.
3 Small bath towels.
1 Nightdress case.
1 Comb bag.
1 Hockey stick (Christmas term).

1 Linen bag.
1 Hair brush.
1 Dress comb.
1 Scurf comb.
1 Workbasket.
1 Lacrosse stick (Easter term).

THE SCHOOL UNIFORM IS SUPPLIED BY

JOHN BARKER and Company, Ltd.

Illustrated Price List on application to the school.

Queen's School, Margate, chose green as its colour and, like most schools in the 1930s, insisted that almost every garment from hat to knickers should be matching. The clothes' list includes all those vanished special items: linen bags, nightdress cases, comb bags and work baskets.

There's a place that is dear to the heart of us,
It is one that has come to be part of us;
It is there we have learn'd to run hard in the race,
Play fair in the field and look life in the face.
O girls, but we'll strive for its honour and fame,
And ever shall we thrill to the sound of its name.

Chorus
Then Hurrah! Hip Hurrah! H.C!
We are proud of the name, H.C.!
Per Ardua ad alta!
Three rousing cheers—H.C.!

In principle, it was hoped that a well-chosen motto would inspire
that esprit de corps so necessary in a school. The romance in the soul
of headmistresses led them to hope, also, that the schoolgirl's reac-
tion to the motto would be a beating heart. This hope was expressed
in the song of the Russell Hill School in Surrey, a private school that
has now merged with its brother-establishment to become co-
educational.

"Non sibi sed omnibus", that is our motto,
Emblazoned on hearts beating high with delight,
It braces the young ones and rouses the old ones,
And strengthens us all for the toil and the fight.

Just so. But the motto wasn't meant just for schooldays. It was for life.
Just as the school song should echo in the memory (as Miss Burstall
put it), so the motto should be a source of strength in later life when
schooldays were over. The song of Trowbridge Girls' High School in
Wiltshire expressed it this way. It was written by the headmistress,
Miss E. Moore, and the music mistress Miss M. E. Trafford.

In after years these words shall be
Our inspiration yet,
To service still, we'll bend our will,
And ever keep through good or ill,
Vigor et Integritas.

In the earlier years, old girls' societies weren't just there for the
purposes of fund raising or nostalgic get-togethers. At a time when
many middle-class girls left school without a profession, they often
went back to home life until they married.

An old girls' society could often offer an interest to these girls, or
as Miss Burstall put it, "The relation of old pupils to their school is an
important part of its social life. They often undertake some special

philanthropic work, independent of the present girls, especially when many have leisure." A school motto could be the rallying cry for these, too. The Thetford Grammar School had a motto "Loyauté me oblige", or "Loyalty binds me". Its school song expected this to apply to old girls as much as to present girls.

> When all of us are scattered
> Upon our several ways,
> And Time creeps on about our Youth
> An ever-deepening haze,
> When other scenes are fading fast
> Beyond our memory,
> Visions of Thetford shall remain.
> Thetford shall still our hearts retain
> In bonds of loyalty,
> In bonds of loyalty.

Esprit de corps was aided by the right clothes. Bentalls, of Kingston-on-Thames, produced this school frock for their 1914 catalogue. It was of navy serge with satin buttons and cost twenty-three shillings and sixpence.

So far most of the mottoes in the school songs have been secular in their nature. Occasionally mottoes turned up in school hymns, as well. The Girls' High School in Wakefield, Yorks, had a hymn written by Canon Edward Welch, and the school's motto, "Each for all and all for God", fitted quite well into it.

> "Each for all" the School's great motto!
> Listen to its clarion call,
> All shall share in each one's honour,
> Shame of one is shame of all.
>
> "All for God" O, Father, make us
> Strong to serve and to endure;
> "All for God" so shall our service
> Singlehearted be and pure.

With mottoes usually went badges and coats of arms. There are a few score girls' schools that have authorised arms from the College of Heralds; but many more simply made up their own unauthorised arms. A less elaborate alternative was to choose a badge and a floral emblem. Nowadays these symbols usually only linger on prize labels, school magazines and trophies. In the early days they were often worn. At Harrogate College, the militancy of the school's motto song was softened by the school's flower song. The flower chosen was the clover, which was embroidered on the breast of every schoolgirl tunic. The girls sang:

Talk not of the queenly rose, nor the stately lily fair;
Take me where the Clover grows with its breath of the glad warm air,
Fragrance of the fields it brings, the meadows are all aglow,
And the Bee its honey sweet distils where the Clover Red doth grow.

Chorus
Clover Red! Clover Red! haunt of the Humble Bee!
Sturdy and straight, emblem of Strength,
Sweetness and Industry.
Ev'ry flow'r hath its hour, but the Clover can never die;
For to each girl here is the Clover dear, and you all know the reason why!

Flowers and girlhood went together. Here the girls of Caldecote Towers cultivate their garden just after the First World War.

At the Skinners' Company's School for Girls the emblem was the rowan tree, and every Prize Day saw the girls dressed in white silk, with sashes, and a bunch of artificial rowan berries. It is the rowan tree that is presumably mentioned in the school song.

> Through wise forethought, long years ago,
> Of an ancient company,
> A seed was sown that should quickly grow
> And flourish mightily.
> Set on the crest of a busy hill,
> And tended with loving care,
> It gathered strength and sweetness, till
> It grew to a tree most rare.
>
> Then for this, the fourth of their school so blest,
> Acclaim them now as winners
> In the planting of schools that will stand all test,
> The Skinners! glorious Skinners.

The same arboreal metaphor turns up in the Oakdene School song. Written by the wife of G. K. Chesterton and still sung, the song has a final line, "Growing in fullness from acorn to oak". The choice of oak presumably comes from the name of the school, but why ivy should be so popular as a school emblem is less obvious. Croydon High School ("The School of the Ivy Green" in its song), chose the ivy leaf emblem; so did Thoresby School.

> O, the ivy is the token of the Thoresby School,
> And Fortis qui se Vincit is our golden rule.
> In all that we may do, our hearts shall still be true
> To the motto that we knew in the Thoresby School.

The rose, of course, was bound to become a school emblem. Queen Anne's, Reading, had it on their badge but it was Clifton High School for Girls, in Bristol, that really took up the rose in a big way. Rose Day, when girls went into the countryside to gather wild roses, was celebrated yearly. Miss M. A. Woods, one of the early headmistresses, wrote a highly romantic song to go with it, which was (understandably) dropped by one of her successors.

> Gather ye roses while ye may,
> The soft May dews are on them,
> The prickles are sharp that block the way,
> But the fearless hand hath won them.
> Rosebud treasures of work and play,
> Harbingers sweet of the unborn day.
> While the young sun-god dozes,
> Gather ye, gather ye roses.

Gather once more though the dim years set,
And the briars be sharp and many,
The rose with the tears of Autumn wet
Methinks is sweeter than any.
Love made pure with a pale regret
And a deathless hope ye shall grasp them yet,
Still ere the brief day closes,
Gather ye, gather ye roses.

One of the best school songs of all comes from Arundel School, Liverpool. Its author, a local clergyman, the Rev. C. C. Elcum, managed to combine pride, humour, the school colours and its flower emblem all in one song. It's a lovely blend of patriotism, fun and girlhoodery. Excluding its chorus, it goes:

You'll see a high building in south Liverpool,
That goes by the name of the Arundel School.
It's largely attended and splendidly run,
And they who know best say it's second to none.

It only takes girls but perhaps by the noise
They make when they're playing you'd think they were boys.
But then they're outside and in school you would say
They work while they work, though they play while they play.

Our chosen school colours are violet hue,
Contrasted with silver stand forth to the view,
To show that where life has a purple background,
There also the silver of hope may be found.

We all for an emblem the violet wear,
'Tis ours to be taught by the blossom we bear.
In eloquent silence it seems to repeat,
"Like me be retiring, be modest, be sweet."

This interpretation of colours—silver for hope, and so forth—is fairly common in school songs. Anybody who has been a schoolgirl between 1920 and 1960 takes it for granted that identification of schools will rest largely on colour—hats, coats, skirts all of the school colour, with matching or carefully contrasting girdles, belts, badges, insignia of prefect rank and so on. Today uniforms are on the way out, but it's still difficult to remember that the original new girls' schools rarely had any uniform at all. Every girl dressed as she liked, though there might be rules limiting materials, styles and hair arrangements. Early photographs of schools before the First World War show a wide variety of dresses.

Uniforms in a sameness of colour found their way into girls' schools via the gymnasium and the games' field. Knickerbockers

School uniform was still the exception in 1900, as this photograph of Caldecote Towers in 1904 shows–seniors are in their own dresses. Doris Worssam, then a little girl at the school, points out that the formidable headmistress, Miss Medina Griffiths, even in those days had her hair cropped.

Below: Gymnasium costume in Bentalls' 1914 catalogue.

and tunics were what Miss Dove had recommended for gym in her chapter in *Work and Play in Girls' Schools*. "That marvellous and cumbersome blue serge pleated tunic, complete with wide velvet collar and huge ribbon bow, long rows of globular brass buttons, knickers coming below the knee, the whole decently covered with a heavy skirt except when we were in the actual gymnasium," is what a 1900 Skinners' girl remembers. Twenty years later, the school had uniform white silk dresses for special occasions, blazers and hats. But it was the tunic and knickerbockers that eventually shrunk into the gymslip with matching knickers. Perhaps it was the ghost of those knickerbockers that lingered on to make the matching knicker of such importance. "We wore green ones called 'jocks' and there were heavy penalties for not having a lining pair, inside, frequently changed," recalled an old girl from Harrogate College. A girl of the Royal Victoria Patriotic School has less happy memories: "Large knickers made of denim which were thick and hot with elastic so tight I thought I would be permanently scarred, under which were worn white liners, equally thick and hot. We changed the blue ones every *three* weeks and the white linings once a week."

The New School Knicker

Lastex Yarn in waist and legs

THE enormous demand we have received for this new knicker (F.144) is indicative of its success and popularity among schools. It has several special features which appeal strongly to all who regard health with the importance it deserves. Instead of the usual elastic which frequently nips and interferes with healthy circulation, we have had a wide band of Lastex yarn knitted in the waist and legs. This clings in a most determined fashion, but without the slightest constriction or pressure. In between the legs, where so much of the wear comes, there is an extra large double gusset. Woven from a two-fold Botany yarn in navy, cream, brown, fawn and green.

Sizes				2	3-4	5-6	7-8
Ages				4-5	6-9	10-13	14-17
Wholesale prices				4/-	4/9	5/6	6/3
Retail prices				4/9	5/6	6/3	7/-

NOTE.—Wholesale prices are quoted for a minimum quantity of 48 garments delivered direct to the School.

The Knicker Lining

A KNICKER lining in hygienic cellular fabric with trunk legs and Lastex waist-band. Designed specially for wear under the above knickers. Easily washed and most comfortable in wear. In cream only (F.265). Sizes 2 to 8 to correspond with knickers. Illustrated in girl's hands.

	All Sizes
Wholesale price	**2/-**
Retail price	**2/6**

NOTE.—The wholesale price is quoted for a minimum quantity of 48 garments delivered direct to the School.

Supergym Stockings

Never fade — Never shrink

IN Supergym stockings we have produced the perfect hose for school wear, for we have eliminated those all-too-common weaknesses of shrinkage, loss of colour and rapid wear into holes.

The method of manufacture is a new one—there being a double process of knitting. Next to the skin is pure Botany wool, while outside is the finest English lisle. The dyeing is also by a new process and the colours are guaranteed absolutely fast.

The stockings have been given the severest tests including every process of washing that is incorrect. For example, a pair of these stockings was placed in a pan of cold water with a mixture of various common soaps. This was brought to the boil and kept boiling for some time. The stockings were then plunged into cold water, wrung out like a floor cloth and finally dried in front of a fire. Yet there were no signs of shrinkage, loss of colour or loss of elasticity. We do not advocate this method of washing, but the test demonstrates the ability of Supergym stockings to withstand the most drastic laundry treatment.

Fully fashioned and spliced throughout with extra reinforcements in the wearing parts, Supergym stockings are extraordinarily durable without any sacrifice of comfort and appearance—and they are fully guaranteed. In school brown, nutria, pine cone, beige and black. Sizes $8\frac{1}{2}$ to $10\frac{1}{2}$ ins. No. E.666.

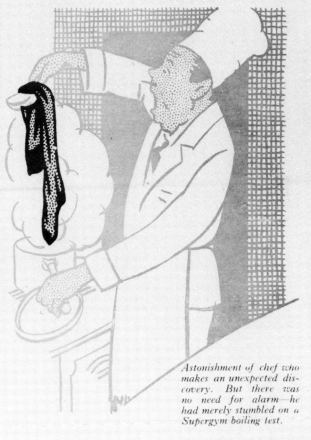

Astonishment of chef who makes an unexpected discovery. But there was no need for alarm—he had merely stumbled on a Supergym boiling test.

Wholesale price	**3/9**	
Retail price	**4/3**	

NOTE.— The wholesale price is quoted for a minimum quantity of 48 pairs delivered direct to the School.

The gymnasium had as much influence on clothes as on health. The girls of Blyth Secondary School, Norfolk, are wearing typical 1936 costume.

Once uniforms were established, matched in colour from knickers to hat bands, the school colours became important. From that point on it was possibly intimately to associate school with its colour scheme. It's not surprising that this close association began to creep into the songs. The George Dixon Girls' Grammar School song entirely identified colours and school:

> On the edge of the city,
> 'Midst meadows green,
> The towers of the school
> To the north are seen.
> Sturdy it stands
> 'Neath a wintry sky
> Unmoved by the winds
> As they whistle by,
> The home of the red and the green.
>
> *Chorus*
> And all who were e'er in the school enrolled
> Shall its name and its fame and its honour uphold.
> Hurrah for the red and the green!

The same colour combination inspired Arthur Waugh, father of Evelyn and Alec. Not far from his home in Hampstead was Frognal School, founded by two ex-members of Roedean's staff and patronised by daughters of the Hampstead élite. Possibly through an acquaintance with some of the parents, Arthur Waugh became the author of the school song. Again, the school colours were red and green, but the song they inspired was smoother and more sophisticated than "Hurrah for the red and the green".

The ubiquitous school knicker reached its peak of influence after the Second World War, when the gym tunic was taken off for gym. Here are some girls from the Commercial Travellers' School, Pinner, in 1956.

All the world over the wandering rover
Wherever his feet may roam,
Binds on his crest the colours that best
Remind him of visions of home.
Gold for the schemer and blue for the dreamer,
But what should we do with these?
For ours are the red of the morning sky,
And the green of the summer trees.
Where Frognal stands on her high hill lands
With her brow to the sun and the breeze.

Chorus
Frognal, Frognal, high on the hill
Where the Hampstead breezes blow,
Hampstead history haunts you still,
With its echoes of long ago.
But the red of the morn on the trees is borne,
Awake, awake, awake!
To life's long story, *Labore, Honore,*
For work and for duty's sake.

Birkenhead Girls' Secondary School, however, would have found matter for complaint in Waugh's song. Their school colours were the very gold and blue he so scornfully dismissed as fit only for schemers and dreamers. Naturally the Birkenhead school song took a different line about the colours' significance.

Gold of the sky, blue of the sea,
What is the message they bear?
Bright blue for hope in the morning of life,
Gold for the joys we renew.

What the well-dressed schoolgirl was wearing in 1937–the Daniel Neal catalogue suggested Collegiate gingham: "As suitable for the schoolroom as the playing field."

STYLE 536. A modern type of games tunic in Collegiate gingham. Bodice has double front and back to ensure a trim tailored appearance, and the full flared skirt provides ample leg freedom.

Lengths 24-26 28-30 32-34 36-38 40-42
| Wholesale Prices | 9/9 | 10/3 | 10/9 | 11/3 | 11/9 |
| Retail Prices | 11/3 | 11/9 | 12/3 | 12/9 | 13/3 |

KNICKERS
| Wholesale price | 3/9 | *All* |
| Retail price | 4/3 | *Sizes* |

STYLE 537. Another modern games tunic in Collegiate gingham. The skirt with its neat pleats allows full freedom of movement and the trim fitting bodice has double front and back.

Lengths 24-26 28-30 32-34 36-38 40-42
| Wholesale Prices | 10/3 | 10/9 | 11/3 | 11/9 | 12/3 |
| Retail Prices | 11/9 | 12/3 | 12/9 | 13/3 | 13/9 |

KNICKERS
| Wholesale price | 3/9 | *All* |
| Retail price | 4/3 | *Sizes* |

STYLE 538. Like the other two styles illustrated this games tunic in Collegiate gingham is as suitable for the schoolroom as the playing field. Skirt has wide box pleat and the square neck bodice has double front and back.

Lengths 24-26 28-30 32-34 36-38 40-42
| Wholesale Prices | 10/- | 10/6 | 11/- | 11/6 | 12/- |
| Retail Prices | 11/6 | 12/- | 12/6 | 13/- | 13/6 |

KNICKERS
| Wholesale price | 3/9 | *All* |
| Retail price | 4/3 | *Sizes* |

Caldecote girls in their gym tunics just after the First World War. Sashes round the waist have become less baggy and skirts somewhat shorter.

In Bath, Miss Bessie Hawkins, head of the Harley Street Junior School, had penned a song which started off "Cling to the old school colours". Its chorus made clear what she thought of gold and green, her particular colours.

> Cling to the old school colours,
> Green for the memories sweet,
> Gold for the chain of friendship
> With its links of love complete.
> Whatever the years may bring us,
> As the leaves of life unfold,
> We will raise a song as we pass along,
> Hurrah for the green and gold!

Red and green, gold and green, gold and blue—almost any combination could be made to echo in the memory. On the whole the themes tended to be similar—friendship, hope, wisdom abounded whether denoted by silver, gold or, as in the Bilston School, Staffordshire, green and grey.

> Now sing we the fame of the green and the grey,
> Let us sing and proclaim it throughout earth today.
> With the name of our school we will make these walls ring;
> Rouse up one and all. Let us sing, let us sing!
>
> The green tells of hope, and we'll never despair,
> Tho' the fates may not smile we will banish dull care.
> We will seek for the wisdom to which our grey calls
> And stand for the truth what e'er befalls.

In the war years, there was a patriotic advantage in brown uniforms. At the Pontefract and District High School, a brown uniform was specifically chosen during this time—brown gymslip, woven sash, shoes, pork-pie hat, and gaberdine coat. Miss Muriel Guest, the English teacher, was at the school at the time, and wrote it a song which drew on the patriotism of wartime schoolgirls.

> We sing a song of schooldays,
> Our school upon the hill.
> Our lessons and our playtime,
> We do them with a will.
> For Oh! we're proud and happy
> To praise our school today.
> As soldiers wear their khaki,
> Its colours we display.
>
> *Chorus*
> Veritas Via Vitae,
> Long live the school.
> Keep its name untarnished,
> That's the schoolgirls' rule.
> May we never shame it,
> Never love it less.
> Good betide it ever,
> P.D.H.S.

Modern schoolchildren in trendy clothes—not a sign of anything matching.

The Convent's Kindly Walls 6

The schoolgirls' rule in a Catholic convent was more than just hon-
ouring the school and keeping its name untarnished. "A Catholic
convent school means omnipresent religion: the rosary said in the
lunch hour during Mary's special months; prayers
before every lesson, grace before meals, visits to the convent
chapel in break time for private prayer, girls from five to eighteen
struggling with their consciences, with the spiritual philosophy of
the Church, believing every childish sin to be a hammer blow on
the nails that pinned Christ to the cross"—this is, above all else,
what Georgina James, a former convent pupil, remembers.

It is not surprising, therefore, that the traditions of the new
high schools—the songs, the coats of arms, the mottoes and the
magazines—should be different in convents. For in the light of a
committed Catholic faith, the ethics of the playing field, "Play up
and play the game", are inadequate. "Forty Years On", with its
mixture of football and muscular Christianity, did not therefore
find favour, and I have not discovered a single convent where it
was sung. Instead every area of tradition became Catholicised.
Coats of arms tended towards doves and lilies; mottoes were usually
religious: magazines had accounts of trips to Lourdes and photographs of the Pope in between news of exams and matches; and
school songs were also mainly religious. Instead of "Forty Years On",
many convents which did not have an individual song, used the
"Holiday Hymn". It provided an infinitely more serious note on
which to end the school year:

> Mother of all that is pure and glad,
> All that is bright and blest,
> As we have taken our toil to Thee,
> So we will take our rest.
> Take Thou and bless our holiday,
> O Causa Nostrae Laetitiae.

Every convent that starts up, unlike a new secular school, has a ready-made tradition—that of the order of nuns that founds it. Thus many convents had a song which belonged rather to the order than to the individual establishment. The Notre Dame Convent in Sheffield used to sing a hymn that honoured St. Julie Billiart, the foundress of their order—a hymn that was also sung at other convents of the same order. It's interesting to see that this is in fact a traditional song of praise to the founder (like many of the songs outside the Catholic tradition), but it has an entirely religious dimension.

> O Notre Dame, the echoes waken
> With praise of Blessed Julie's name;
> From her own song our keynote taking,
> Deep in each heart sweet music making,
> "The good God is so very good"
> We sing,
> "The good God is so very good."

The pupils of Our Lady's School, 1896. Later the school became the Convent of the Sacred Heart, Queen's Cross, Aberdeen.

While the heroines and inspiration of the secular or Church of England schools were generally either famous men and women, or even the original headmistress, in convents the human model for pupils was usually a saint. "Noble friendships with the saints in glory," wrote Janet Erskine Stuart in *The Education of Catholic Girls*, 1912, "are one of the most effectual means of learning heavenly-mindedness, and friendships formed in childhood will last throughout a lifetime." At St. Mary's Convent, Mount Battenhall, Worcester, the school song sums it up:

> Proudly our voice we raise,
> In songs of joy and praise,
> To honour our School, which we love and revere.
> Here where we work and play,
> Nearer to God each day,
> With Mary our model and patroness dear.

From a women's liberation point of view, the advantage of this was that there were many female saints to give a female model for the schoolgirl. This meant that songs could adapt well to girls, and that convent pupils did not find themselves in the anomalous position of singing about "men"—as if their own existence was subsumed in the male sex. The variety of saints meant that one could always be found to exemplify whatever virtues the convent wished to emphasise. "The names of Matilda of Tuscany, of St. Catherine of Sienna, of Blessed Joan of Arc, of Isabella the Catholic, of St. Theresa are representative amongst others of women who have fulfilled public missions for the service of the Church . . . Others have reigned in their own sphere in families, or solitudes, or cloistered enclosures—as the two Saints Elizabeth, Paula and Eustochium and all their group of friends, the great Abbesses Hildegarde, Hilda, Gertrude and others", wrote Janet Erskine Stuart.

And if one included all the potential male saints, there was no shortage of models. A gentle patron saint, like St. Thérèse of Lisieux, meant a gentle convent song—like this one from the Ursuline Convent School in Blundellsands, Liverpool:

> Though a little school and lowly,
> Lofty is our aim.
> We yield to none in striving
> For the glory of God's name.
> We hold aloft our banners
> And fearless all toils face:
> The Little Flower all overcame
> When she trod in Our Lady's trace.

At the other extreme was the inspiration of St. Dominic, patron of the Dominican convents both in Britain and South Africa, where a militant song was adopted, suitable for the saint. Its author, Sister M. Xavier Cullen, died in South Africa only a few years ago, and nowadays the song is not always sung.

Far away in time and distance,
Out of every clime and land,
Dominic, the warrior-hero,
Called to him his white-robed band.
So we give him meed of honour,
The hero of our youth,
For our convent school, St. Dominic's,
Bears his championship of truth.

Chorus
On our uniforms of crimson,
See the badge's clear design.
May our lives be in accordance
And their honour brightly shine.
Mid the dust and din around us
May our school name pass.
To St. Dominic—to our school and convent home,
Pledge we—VERITAS.

The May procession in honour of Our Lady by the girls of St. Monica's Convent, Skipton. "We had the great unifying experience of shared worship," recalls Betty McEntegart, one of these 1940 pupils, "either in the Convent chapel, or, as on Sundays, in the parish church."

Like other schools, convents also valued the virtues of loyalty and patriotism. Saints could adapt to this role as well. The St. Joan of Arc School in Rickmansworth had a particularly patriotic song—despite the undeniable fact that its patron saint had been a successful warrior *against* the British.

Ring clearly, bells, from day's bright dawning,
Sing sweetly, birds, throughout the sky.
Oh hills and seas and stars of all time,
Our patron Saint proclaim on high.
All ye who seek truth and who fight with brave hearts,
For Saint Joan and her standard true,
The fleur-de-lys our shield against the foe's darts,
Advance and fight the battle through!

Chorus
Joan of Arc for the love we bear thee,
We pledge to keep our fair standard free,
For God, for home, for country and for friends,
Fidelitas pro patria,
Fidelitas fraternitas,
Fidelitas ad omnia,
Fidelis ad Mortem.

The same patriotism, mingled with a lyrical description of the convent's surroundings, is found in the school song of St. Monica's Convent, Skipton, York. Sister Milburga Kay, its author, wrote this romantic verse to the school.

Our Alma Mater lies beside a castle famed of yore,
Not distant far an Abbey stands alone on Wharfe's green shore,
Around us stretch the moorlands bleak, the heath and rugged hills,
Where blows a brave and vig'rous air and silvery shine the rills.

Chorus
St. Monica, St. Monica, so train us 'neath thy rule,
That we in one strong love may hold—
God, Country, Home and School.

The intimacy found in the smaller schools of an earlier age was particularly marked in convents. A former convent pupil recalls: "I suppose my main impression is one of total girlishness. Our wrestlings with philosophical religious questions gave us a mental toughness beyond our years. But we were naive in terms of worldly wisdom. Our society was so safe, so ordered, that we could trust and be honest without fear of deception." Rituals of this ordered world could be remembered for decades. Mrs. Norah Hampson, who went to St. John's parish school in Wigan in 1909 when it was run by the Jesuits, recalled: "I can see Sister Mary Joseph now standing on a little platform, doing the same actions every day. First in the morning, lighting a lamp before a picture of the Holy Face on Veronica's towel, which hung by her desk. As she did this the glass partitions were open and the whole school and teachers stood in silence. On feast days we sang 'Dear old St. John's'." Its chorus went:

> Hearty and strong to you,
> Dear old St. John's,
> Rises our song to you,
> Dear old St. John's.
> Let the full chorus tell
> How your own love you well,
> Proud to belong to you,
> Dear old St. John's.

Some of the virtues emphasised in convent songs would not usually be so stressed in secular schools. Purity in particular was valued. Taken to excess, this could mean a benevolently authoritarian regime—no private letters, constant supervision, extraordinary bathing rituals. Mrs. Catherine Hardy can remember, like many other pre-war convent pupils, the obsession with modesty in the bathtub. "Although the nuns nowadays are broadminded, in the 1930s they were excessively prudish. The small girls up to about eight or nine years were bathed by a young nun, but we used to have to wear a swimsuit. There were only about three suits, so those who did not get one of the dry ones had to put on a wet one." Other convent girls recollect bathing in voluminous white garments rather like nighties. But the value set upon chastity and purity had its inspirational moments, too. St. Joseph's Convent Grammar School in Abbey Wood, South-East London, was founded in 1904 and given the motto "Potius Mori Quam Foedari", Death rather than Dishonour. "The legend is that the ermine when hunted can easily be taken if driven towards muddy marshy land," explained Sister Mary Dominic, author of the school song, written round this motto. "It will turn to face death rather than soil its white coat." The song was still in use in 1976, when the school was facing merger into a large comprehensive co-educational establishment. The last grammar school pupils sang:

> Model our lives on thee, O motto dear,
> Honour and Purity shall conquer Fear.
> Honour unstained and bright, guarded by thee,
> Until there dawns at last, Eternity.

> Honour and Purity shall guard our way,
> Shining 'mid shades of night till dawn of day.
> Through childhood's happy hours, through life's long years,
> Girls of St. Joseph's School shall know no fears.

The security that came from these absolute values had its jolly side. Convent life may have had its repressions: it was also full of fun. Something about the very innocence of it all lent excitement to childish games. In these games, the high point was reached if it involved a friendly priest. "Sometimes a Jesuit priest would come in, and we would say prayers and Sister made us go on the stage and do a turn for him. We all sang 'Here we go Luby-Loo', priest and all, and he would fall over as he put his leg up, and we all would try to pull him up." The innocent games of 1909 are still remembered. Another convent girl has never forgotten thrilling and terrifying games of Dracula in the shrubbery, with the local parish priest playing the part of the great Undead.

A great moment for the pupils of Queen's Cross—the bishop's visit. Note that these 1951 pupils are wearing white gloves, compulsory on all solemn occasions.

When outside educational influences found their way into songs, they were often softened and made more intimate. At the Ursuline High School for Girls in Ilford, the school song, now no longer used, was reminiscent of Henry Newbolt's "Best School of All". But the best school of all, tellingly, became the dearest school of all.

> We raise a song of grateful praise
> For every happy day
> We spend within these kindly walls
> At eager work and play.
> For training true of mind and will,
> For blessings great and small,
> How shall we pay the debt we owe
> To the dearest school of all?

School, indeed, had something of a home atmosphere. Sometimes, of course, this was a survival from the Victorian select boarding school for girls—the very image that the new high schools and public schools were trying to get away from. But at its best, a good convent could combine both intimacy and excellent teaching—the reservoir of dedicated and educated women was there in the convent's order. St. Bernard's Convent, Westcliff-on-Sea, has a song by Jenny Boland that equates school with home.

> Sing we the house that we all love so dearly,
> St. Bernard's the home of our life's brightest years.
> Sing out its praises both loudly and cheerly,
> And pray it may flourish for many long years.
>
> There we have all lived in happy relation,
> Performing our tasks as a pleasure, not care.
> So let us keep up the great reputation,
> A child of St. Bernard's is known everywhere.

At St. Bernard's, as at other convents, concerts and entertainments were regularly given for the Reverend Mother, who was held in an awed affection. At the La Sagesse Convent High School in Newcastle upon Tyne, there was a special song for Reverend Mother's feast day, calling on her patron saint.

> Glory and praise to St. Joseph,
> Guardian of God's holy life,
> Protector of Jesus and Mary
> In peace and when danger was rife.
> Praise to our own Reverend Mother
> Who bears his name today,
> That God may protect and preserve her,
> Thus we do pray.

At the Holt Hill Convent Grammar School, Birkenhead, both Reverend Mother and the headmistress were honoured on their feast days. The headmistress had a fairly short song:

> Vivat, vivat, vivat, Mater Bona,
> Vivat, vivat, ad multos annos.
> List to our festal lay,
> We sing with joy today.
> Our hearts and voice upraise
> To wish you happy days.

DIEM MON ABRI

CONCERT

offered to

REVEREND MOTHER

St BERNARD'S   VIVAT   JULY 2nd 1936

St. Bernard's Convent held regular entertainments for the Reverend Mother, before the Second World War. Carefully painted programmes, often with special lettering inside, were produced for these important occasions.

A charming example
of how almost every
area of school life
becomes Catholicised
in a convent. The
Prize Day programme
is done with
illuminated lettering,
like that of a medieval
manuscript.

PRIZE~DAY

JULY 26.1933

S.T BERNARDS

CONVENT

HIGH SCHOOL

VIVAT

M·Cullen.

The bond between pupil and Mother Superior was a stronger one than that between pupil and teacher. The Reverend Mother, after all, was a spiritual superior, indeed, a spiritual mother—a forceful idea in a faith that places emphasis upon the Virgin Mother of Christ. So it is not surprising to find that the Holt Hill convent song for the Reverend Mother was rather more elaborate than the one for the headmistress. Its first verse went:

> All hail to this bright festal day!
> God bless you, Reverend Mother dear,
> While we beneath your loving gentle sway
> Bring you our greetings most sincere.
> O Mother loved, we wish you joy today,
> With grateful hearts we sing our festal lay.
> A happy feast we wish you, Mother,
> And may God bless your coming year.

Not all memories of Mother Superiors are happy ones. Elizabeth Hogg recalls singing her convent song on the Reverend Mother's feast day with less than enthusiasm. "She always sat surrounded by flowers on a chair on the dais smiling grimly and beating out of time to the music (she was both tone-deaf and irrhythmic) while Miss Gunterden played the piano and we belted out the song. Miss G. played with enormous gusto and her style resembled that of a swimming dog."

Early pupils of the Sacred Heart Convent, Queen's Cross, Aberdeen, all with immaculate white dresses and black stockings. Shoes are stout and sensible in 1898.

Even on the playing fields there was a tendency for convents to be slightly different from secular schools. On the whole, the extremes of the games obsession did not flourish in convents and no hockey, tennis or cricket songs have come to light. The song nearest in spirit to the hearty ethics of Roedean, Wycombe Abbey or St. Andrew's comes from the Convent of the Sacred Heart, Queen's Cross, Aberdeen. In the 1960s the whole school was divided into two houses, blues and golds. The highest honour, reports Alison MacKintosh, was a round enamel badge with either a pale blue I on it, or a gold V. The significance of these initial letters is clear from the convent song written by Molly Grant:

> Intrepid Blues and Valiant Golds,
> Come sing of our school today,
> Of the victories won and the best we have done
> In the hours of our work and play.
> As the years roll on and old memories throng,
> And the words that we sing in our hearts may ring
> With an echo courageous and gay,
> Borne afar from the grey North Sea
> Aberdeen and Saint Andrew our slogan shall be.
>
> *Chorus*
> For some have brought thee honour and fame,
> But one and all we've played the game.
> Then raise, raise the song on high,
> Queen's Cross for Aye,
> Queen's Cross for Aye,
> Aberdeen for ever.

The convent was unusually enthusiastic about games. Baseball was taken so seriously that Alison MacKintosh recalls no less than four daily sessions of it. Why hockey, tennis and netball should have come only a very poor second is not clear. But in *The Education of Catholic Girls* comes a passage which (if it fails to explain baseball), does at least give a clue to why convents should have produced no hockey songs. "It is worth attention that some games, as hockey, conduce to all the attitudes and movements which are least to be desired, and that others as basketball, on the contrary, tend—if played with strict regard to rules—to attitudes which are in themselves beautiful and tending to grace of movement." Hockey in some way had got itself a bad name in those early Catholic educational circles.

The only other convent song in which I have discovered a trace—and only a trace—of the "Play up and play the game" spirit belongs to the Sionian convents. Sister Marie Pancratius wrote it around 1934 for Our Lady of Sion School in West London, and it was subsequently adopted by Our Lady of Sion School, Holloway and the Sion Senior School in Worthing. Sister Marie's rousing song is quite secular in tone.

> Carry on the Sionian Tradition,
> It comes down from the years that are gone,
> And the voices of past generations
> Are now calling to us "Carry on!"
> For the future will be what we make it,
> As we work, as we play in our day,
> We will keep the torch burning and pass it on
> As a light to show others the way.

A certain militancy is often found in convent songs. In the high schools and public schools, militant aggression usually refers to the fights on the playing fields, or possibly is used in the context of patriotism. In convents, the militancy is again a question of religion. Life, indeed, is no playing field. It is a battleground of Right and Wrong, a metaphor with some 2000 years of use behind it. Notre Dame High School in Crownhill, Plymouth, has one of the most charmingly militant songs.

> We have fallen in line with the troops that go,
> Notre Dame still strong abreast:
> They have marched far ahead, and the rear is filled,
> There's no dropping out for a rest.
> With the bugle note so keen,
> And a cry that long has been:
> We will live, Notre Dame, for your endless name.
> We will live and die for our Queen.

Sister Julie Alphonse, the author, in 1927 did not make a conscious choice of a military theme. "It was just a matter of inspiration rising from the particular place and the 'feel' of the school at the time. Most of the pupils belonged to naval or military backgrounds . . . Clearly a military kind of song would be taboo in English society today. At the time of writing, however, ideas and words rose naturally to my heart and aural senses," she explained.

This serious outlook on life was not confined to Catholic girls. Protestant girls were, and are, often educated in convents and rarely made to feel either unwelcome or different. At La Sainte Union Convent in Highgate, London, the song had this to say about convent education:

> You taught us the dangers to come on the morrow,
> The trials and the joys of the way to be trod—
> You gave us a shield 'gainst all pain and all sorrow
> For each is for all, yes, and all is for God.

Its fifteen-year-old schoolgirl author, Joyce Rowe, later published poetry in many periodicals. The Reverend Mother asked her to compose the words, giving her carte blanche to do as she thought best, even though she was a Protestant.

Finally the convent, as well as being a home for girls of other faiths, could also encompass many nationalities. At the Loreto College, Manchester, Monica Whitfield, a pupil in the 1930s, can remember the feeling of belonging to an international organisation as they sang these words from a song by Alfred Mistowski, written for Loreto convents everywhere:

> To East and West of that fair Isle where the first Loreto stands,
> Loreto's banner now doth fly in many lands, in many distant lands.
> In sunny, sunny Spain, on Afric's strand,
> Under the Southern Cross,
> And Westward Ho, where rainbow-hued
> Niagara's waters cross.

Songs of Empire

7

In the old world of schoolgirl song, there was not only Great Britain but also the Empire, stretching across the world and colouring a lot of the map a nice warm red. Empire Day was celebrated with fervour—usually with a Union Jack well to the fore, some marching, and a stirring speech from the headmistress. At Bath's Harley Street Junior School, there was a procession of small girls through the city, and a specially-made-up song ('Honour the Land we love, girls') was sung to mark the occasion. Its enthusiastically patriotic refrain ended:

> Honour the King whose Empire
> Stretches across the sea,
> Proud of the name Britain can claim,
> True British girls are we.

All over the globe other schoolgirls were going through similar celebrations, for the heyday of the school song was also the heyday of the Empire. Like the red on the map, the girls' school song spread from continent to continent, bringing enlightenment (sometimes bewilderment) to the native inhabitants. High on the Himalayan slopes of the North Punjab in the 1920s, Alice Steane can remember singing:

> Ghora Gali is our Alma Mater:
> Cheer for the Lawrence School.
> Colonel Wright is our well-loved Pater,
> Happy those 'neath his rule.
> We're proud of our School,
> And all things in it,
> And we'll tell you why in half a minute.
> But first in your ears we'll din it—
> Cheer for the Lawrence School.

The Lawrence College at Ghora Gali was a proper girls-only school, with its brother establishment for boys some safe two miles away. A few Anglo-Indian girls were admitted but pupils were mainly the daughters of Indian Army officers. There were hockey, guides,

Girl guide troops flourished in girls' schools all over the world, enriching the schoolgirl repertoire with their own songs such as "The Mango Walk", "Scrape No Fiddlestick", and "The Swiss Chalet Song". These and other campfire favourites were sung by the Caldecote Towers troop, pictured here in 1919 with their banner.

houses, Cambridge examinations, Speech Day, chapel and everything that should be. The only difference from the schools back home was the exotic setting of the Himalayan pinewoods, the Indian fowl, the earthquakes, and, at night, the howling of the jackals.

In Burma, Patricia Sanglier can remember the proud song of the Methodist English Girls' High School, in Signal Pagoda Road, Rangoon, with its stirring end of verse:

> Rah! Rah! Rah!
> Watch us as we climb to fame and glory,
> We are here for victory.
> Oh, give a yell, oh, as ever on we go,
> Three cheers for the Methodist Girls' High School!

While in the hot climate of Lagos, Miss Dorothy Peel in the 1930s decided to write a song for Queen's College, the only government secondary school for girls in Nigeria at the time. "When I joined the staff there was no school song, only a motto, 'Pass on the Torch'. I suggested writing a song when my friend, the police bandmaster, volunteered to do the music. I think I adapted the words chiefly to virtues I myself valued," she admits. The result, sung up to a year or two ago and possibly still in use, started:

> Pass on the torch still brightly gleaming,
> Pass on the hopes, the earnest dreaming
> To those who follow close at hand.
> Pass on the thoughts, the skill, the learning,
> Pass on the secret inmost yearning
> That they may build where we have planned.

Girls' school songs had become established even earlier in the "white" colonies. By the second half of the last century they were springing up all over the place. Indeed, it's interesting to see that quite a few of the schools in South Africa and Australia have foundation dates which rank as early as those, say, of the Girls' Public Day School Trust. Some indeed are even earlier. As early as 1860 six German missionaries in Stellenbosch, Cape Province of South Africa, set up accommodation for a girls' boarding school, later the Rhenish Girls' School. The school had a special hymn "O God of Bethel", a psalm, and a Biblical motto "Ebenezer" which means "Hitherto the Lord hath helped us". Its song is only twenty years old, but Miss J. Jenkins, the staff member who wrote it, has summed up in its lines the essential loyalties of the schoolgirl world.

> We may not all be brilliant
> In sport not all do well,
> But the hope of each and all of us
> Is that Rhenish may excel.
> Ebenezer is our watchword,
> For our school our hearts beat strong.
> "God guide our eager footsteps
> Sing praise to this our song."

Girls' schools in the Colonies, like St. Mary's Girls' College in New Zealand, clung to the old traditions. Their 1929 uniform could just as well have been worn at Cheltenham, or the Wigan Girls' High School.

99

The other early foundation, from which I have culled a song, is in New South Wales, Australia. Willoughby Girls' High School can date its origins from before 1867 when a small school with thirty children was in existence. It took another sixty-nine years before the school acquired its own song with the rousing last lines:

> Our colours true of white and blue, we'll wear and wave on high
> With pride to show how much we owe to High School Willoughby.

Quite a few of the early schools looked to England for the founding staff. The Eunice High School in Bloemfontein, South Africa, was started in 1875, and its first principal Miss E. Laird came out from Scotland specially for the job. "The school's name, 'Eunice', is derived from the Greek 'Happy Victory' and also refers to Eunice, the mother of St. Timothy, to whose 'unfeigned faith' tribute was paid by St. Paul in his epistle to Timothy," explains the school's current headmistress, Mrs. J. M. Posthumus. Its song is also relatively early, being composed by Miss E. L. M. King, headmistress from 1913 onwards.

> Though all around has chang'd since her corner-stone was laid,
> The spirit of Eunice has never been dismayed.
> The future will not fright her, she fears nor change nor strife,
> For she dwells beside the waters of wisdom and of Life.

Some of the early schools were founded in conscious imitation of English foundations. Names like Girton and Roedean, for instance, crop up in Australian schools, while in Durban the Girls' College was founded in imitation of Cheltenham Ladies' College in 1877. The school has rather a romantic song which refers to the ship on the school badge. It was written by June Drummond, now known as an author, but then only a sixteen-year-old schoolgirl.

> All hail the College Galleon
> Dim freight of dreams she bears,
> Through rich and glorious yesterday
> Towards tomorrow's years.
> Golden with promise her ports of call
> Eager her crew and free,
> Borne on the carefree wings of youth
> Across uncharted sea.

Some songs even commemorate the first pioneer settlers. Avonside Girls' High School in Christchurch, New Zealand, took, as names of its four houses in the 1930's, the names of the first four ships that

Conscious imitation of the British girls' schools can perhaps be detected in this early picture of Wellington Girls' College, New Zealand. The buildings, though slightly colonial in style, still have the inevitable school tower, an architectural feature designed for morale rather than use.

brought settlers to Canterbury in 1850. Aotea-Roa is the old Maori name for New Zealand. The song, which is no longer in use partly because, among other changes, there are now 1100 pupils—too many for just four houses—was written by two pupils, Nancy Hitchcock and Dorothy Neal. Its second verse went:

> To Aotea-Roa the pioneers came,
> With high ideals and true, their English hearts aflame,
> May their ideals be ours today,
> Whatever Fortune's tide,
> For Seymour, Cressy, Charlotte Jane
> And Randolph of Avonside.

Neither antipodean nor South African schools seem to have gone in for complete school songbooks, like Girton, Wycombe Abbey and St. Andrew's back in the homeland. Indeed, the songs seem to have come mainly in the second, third or fourth generation of headmistresses' time. The Church of England Girls' Grammar School, the Hermitage, Geelong, is an exception. This Australian private school had a song written for it early on in its life. The Hermitage, as it was known from its building, was always rather posh. Its first headmistress, Elsie Morres—not unlike the Miss Lawrence of Roedean in her keenness—created a school of a decidely sporty type. The local vicar, a whimsical cleric called the Rev. Alfred Wheeler, in about 1908 volunteered to write the music, and Miss Agnes Cross, one of a loyal staff, wrote the words. The result was a marvellous antipoedean version, which adapted all the jolliness and seriousness of the British school song into an essentially Australian form.

> Australia's own call to her daughters
> Is the call of your school now as well;
> May its echoes ring cheerily round you,
> Making feelings of gratitude swell.
> May it be that your conduct will aye prove your worth,
> Of your love for your School and the land of your birth,
> Coo-ee, Coo-ee! Long live the School.
>
> May lessons you learn in your school days
> Through life make your path ever bright;
> May you grow in all virtue and beauty
> Gentle, honest and strong in the right.
> In all games that you play, in all work that you do,
> Do the work, play the game, as a girl straight and true.
> Coo-ee! Coo-ee! Long live the School.

"Do the work, play the game, as a girl straight and true". Physical education in New Zealand schools in 1945. Note the traditional navy-blue knickers.

"Coo-ee", that aboriginal cry, was also the name of the school magazine. Alas, neither it nor the school is extant today. With the possible exception of South Africa, the schools on the other side of the globe to Britain are equally threatened, both by the fashion for co-education and, if they are private, by inflation. "Coo-ee" had to close because the Hermitage found it was losing pupils to co-educational establishments. The school merged with two other private schools to form a new co-educational establishment. Even in New Zealand, where almost all the girls-only schools are state run, co-education looms. "I hope we survive to be a hundred," wrote the Waitaki Girls' High School principal, Joyce Jarrold, "but I can see the co-ed take-over coming." Waitaki High School, in Oamaru, has a particularly jolly school song written in 1935 by Marjorie Mowat, one of the pupils.

> Green the fields that lie around
> Waitaki's stately walls,
> Gay our happy laughter's sound,
> Echoing thro' the halls.
>
> *Chorus*
> Alma Mater! Alma Mater!
> Sing we songs of love and praise.
> Oh Waitaki! Oh Waitaki!
> Mother of our girlhood days.
>
> Schooldays over, pastimes call,
> Sports are to the fore,
> Tennis, swimming, basketball—
> All of these and more.

The sentiments, particulary the joyful appreciation of school games, are the same as in British schools. It's interesting, too, to find this emphasis slightly more pronounced in private schools. In Australia, Elsie Moores of the Hermitage was largely responsible (so the school's history claims) for making sport for women an accepted part of the school curriculum. Another private school, St. Catherine's in Toorak, Victoria, took to it with great enthusiasm. To the ever-useful tune of *John Peel,* the St. Catherine's schoolgirls sung this dauntless song.

> St. Catherine's girls, St. Catherine's girls,
> Where'er the flag of right unfurls,
> With our banner of blue and our motto true,
> Learn to play the game in life's morning.

Our badge is blue with a golden gleam,
You will see it shine when you meet our team;
And we'll prove our mettle on life's great field,
And go home with our colours flying.

St. Catherine's first will play the game,
And when we fall will try again;
And fight for truth and the School's good name,
With effort never tiring.

*St. Catherine's girls
proving their mettle
on the playing fields
in the 1940s.*

The enthusiasm for the playing fields is the same whatever the continent: so is the keenness on the school colours. The Firbank Church of England Girls' Grammar School, in Brighton, Victoria, used to sing:

So sing our songs that the echoes may go
To the old girls far and near;
Till they long for their schooldays over again
And the colours they used to wear.
So girls of today, if in years to come,
You wish to feel the same,
You'll fight for the colours and love the School,
And always play the game.

Exercises in the gymnasium were as important in early colonial schools as back home. This early photograph shows the pupils of Wellington Girls' College displaying their skills.

Across the ocean in New Zealand, the old song of Wanganui Girls' College used to praise the school's colours of blue and gold. It was written by a staff member, Miss K. Browning, an old Girtonian, in 1903. Possibly she remembered the songs of Girton College.

The blue it stands for heaven,
The gold for honour bright,
And symbol of our College
Is the pride of the starry night.
Wherever we may wander
Wherever we may roam,
The starry sky above us
Will tell of school and home.

Jollity abounds in Australian songs. Sydney Girls' High School's song about their colours was undoubtedly particularly uninhibited. It's been somewhat tamed for the modern version, but in old days the girls would sing:

Girls who wear the brown and yellow
Stand in line, each by her fellow,
Sweetly sing or loudly bellow
Sydney Girls' High School!

The last full verse, also not used now, refers to Vigoro, a sort of cricket with oval bats and a rubber ball. The school's principal, Miss D. M. Shackley, maintains that it's a faster game than cricket but has lost popularity lately in the school.

Vigoro and tennis claim us,
Basketball and hockey lame us,
But our sports' team ne'er will shame us;
Long live the Girls' High School.
Some girls study Classics, others Mathematics,
Botany, Geology and Chemistry and even Hydrostatics;
Some are dunces, some are clever,
Destiny our lives may sever,
Flourish now and flourish ever,
Sydney Girls' High School!

Cricket, or possibly even vigoro, in front of the Wellington Girls' College, New Zealand.

Handicrafts (left) *and home science* (right) *were by 1948 firmly established upon the New Zealand curriculum. Formality, however, still reigned in the kitchen, where pupils not only dress in aprons, but also wear nun-like wimples.*

It's stirring stuff, as is the song which comes from the Girls' High School in Napier, New Zealand. Written in 1926, it's still sung, though there's a school hymn for rather more serious occasions.

> Come, let us all be jolly,
> And whatever may befall,
> Let us banish melancholy,
> And answer Learning's call.
> Each day is swiftly gliding,
> And our work we have to do,
> There must be no back-sliding,
> From the girls of the White and the Blue.

It's a nice idea that learning can banish melancholy—obviously shared by the girls of Sydney Church of England Grammar School, whose motto is *Luceat Lux Vestra* (" Let your light shine"). Muddling the metaphors a bit, they used to sing:

> Your lamp may light you to hard mental toil,
> Your distaff reel with Science's great coil,
> Often, maybe, you'll burn youth's midnight oil—
> *Luceat Lux Vestra.*

In South African schools, especially, great emphasis seems to have been laid on sport. Johannesburg High School for Girls has a song which suggests why this may have occurred:

> We've a Bath for swimming and a Hall for "gymn,"
> For we must be supple and fleet of limb
> In a land where such sports are conducted in style
> By the springbok, ostrich and crocodile;
> And at seasons proper we stake our fate
> On a contest grim but devoid of hate,
> And we cheer the victors with this refrain;
> *"Vincemus! Vincemus!* We'll win yet again."

That refrain was mild on the playing field compared with some. Boksburg High School has a particularly blood-curdling series of war cries for sporting occasions, including this:

> Hold him down, you Boksburg Warrior chief, chief, chief.
> Hi-nicker, Deema, Deema, Deema, Day.
> Hold him down, you Boksburg Warrior King.

There's also a chant, where each line is repeated twice, which ends up with a terrifying shout.

> We've done the thing
> And you'll hear us sing,
> And your ears will ring
> And when we win,
> You'll hear the din.
> Bokburg, Bok, Bok, Bok, Bok.

It's only surpassed in fervour by the chant of Parktown High School for Girls. Oddly enough, but for the one exception of Walthamstow High School, I have found these chants only in South African schools. The playing fields of Australia and New Zealand remain silent. One of the Parktown High School chants is borrowed from the brother school, Parktown Boys' High, who adapted Zulu words for the playing fields.

> *Prefects*
> U Kula muna banee
>
> *School*
> U Kula muna seebee
>
> *All together*
> Zing, ting nigating
> Ee la vous.

P A R K—Zimba, zimba, zimba, yeh!
T O WN—Zimba, zimba, zimba, you!
P A R K T O W N

This perhaps shows the influence of American cheer leading. But there's also a good chant which belongs and has always belonged to the girls' school alone.

As we shout our War Cry
On the day of Inter High,
As we shout and we scream
And we cheer on our team,
As we shout "Who are we?"
"We are we"—
A B C D E F G H I J K L M N O P A R K T O W N !
Parktown!

More sober songs, of course, are found. Rustenburg High School, Cape Town, contents itself with:

Then here's to the Powers among us,
And here's to the classrooms cool,
Hurrah for the Past and the Present,
Hurrah for our famous school!

The school song, indeed, of Riebeek College Girls' High School, Uitenhage, is positively gentle.

All hail be to our College,
The College we all know.
Her good name will follow
Wherever we may go.
In times of need remember
All that she stands for best,
Ora et Labora will always
Stand the test.

It's perhaps worth pointing out that these are all-white songs. I have not found a single school song that belongs to girls' schools for either black or coloured pupils in South Africa. But I have discovered one rather ingenious version of *Forty Years On*. It's not quite the same song, but surely the "Follow on" of the Collegiate School for Girls, Port Elizabeth, is an echo of "Follow up".

Girls of the College, girls of the College,
Girls of the games club who stand here today,
Stiff is our climb up the steep hill of knowledge,
Stiff, too, our climb up the stout hill of play.
Nothing in life's to be won without trying,
Strength of the body and vigour of soul.
Old Father Tempus is flying, is flying,
Let us fly after and win to our goal.
Follow on, follow on, follow on, follow on, follow on.
Let us follow the old College cry,
For it's *Facta non Verba* for aye.

The other echo came from Girton College, in Mackenzie Street, Bendigo, Victoria—the antipodean namesake of Miss Emily Davies' rose-red Gothic pile outside Cambridge. Girton College doesn't have the wealth of song of its British counterpart but it does have a rather nice school song:

We'll honour still the ones who taught us,
Goals to strive for, fights to win,
We'll carry high the torch they brought us,
Keep the flame from growing dim.
Down the halls of time they guide us,
Stars above us, truth within.

Across the globe, in the heat of the antipodean sun, the jungles of India, the wildest bush of Africa, the schoolgirl spirit is still playing the game.

The end of term was also the time for school plays–the girls of the Perse High School, Cambridge, did Julius Caesar *in 1930.*

Golden Days We Shall Never Forget

8

The triumph and glory of the school song came on Speech Day, or Prize Day, or whatever was the name given to the yearly celebration. The whole school was gathered together, with proud mothers and fathers looking on, distinguished guests on the dais of the school assembly hall, and a sprinkling of old girls down to celebrate the end of the scholastic year. It was an occasion for silk, or tussore, or shantung frocks a generation ago, for carefully matching hair ribbons and, of course, white gloves. And for the generation before that there had been hats, and probably some kind of flower pinned onto the sashes.

This emotional moment is rarely forgotten. "We all had to have for this occasion a prize-giving dress in white jap silk with a long emerald green ribbon at the throat," recollects an Abbey School old girl. "When we were crammed together tier upon tier behind the platform of the Great Hall of Reading University, somebody, once told the headmistress that we looked like a bed of lilies." For schools lucky enough to have their own assembly halls, there would be the evocative honours boards all around, recalling past prize-winners, as the present winners, glowing with pride and trepidation, went to collect their trophies—those odd cups, shields, badges, coloured ribbons, sometimes even tiepins that were treasured through the subsequent years. As the song of Howell's School, Denbigh, put it:

> As we meet in the halls whose memory recalls
> The names of our heroes of yore,
> Our hearts beating high with pride and with joy
> As we mass in the long corridor . . .

There were always weeks of patient rehearsal. The school choir would be put through its paces again and again. The whole school would practise filing in—in exactly the right order and woe betide the head of form who led the wrong way. There would be inspections on the great day to make sure every girl was properly dressed, and last

Clothing list for Howell's School, Denbigh. Appropriately enough for a school founded by a member of the Drapers' Company, clothes were of expensive material. "When I was there from 1934 to 1938", recollects Mrs. Sybil Tope, "the uniform changed from shantung frocks to grey pinafore dresses, and divided skirts were introduced for the first time."

FOR SUMMER ONLY.

1 Shantung Frock.

Lengths :	30″	33″	36″	39″	42″	45″	48″
	30/5	32/5	34/5	36/5	38/5	40/5	42/5

1 Shantung Petticoat, round neck (optional).

Lengths :	30″	33″	36″	39″	42″	45″	48″
	8/9	9/3	9/9	10/3	10/9	11/3	11/6

1 Pair Shantung Knickers.

Lengths :	14″	16″	18″	20″	22″	24″
	5/3	5/6	5/9	6/-	6/3	6/6

2 Gingham Frocks (Seniors).

Lengths :	40″	42″	44″	46″	48″
	14/6	14/9	15/-	15/3	15/6

2 Knickers to match.

	18″	20″	22″	24″
	2/9	3/-	3/3	3/6

2 Gingham Frocks (Juniors).

Lengths :	26″	28″	30″	32″	34″	36″
	13/3	13/6	13/9	14/-	14/3	14/6

2 Knickers to match.

Sizes :	14″	16″	18″	20″
	2/3	2/6	2/9	3/-

Gingham Material, 31″, 1/- per yard. For those parents wishing to make the frocks at home.

1 Bathing Costume at 11/6. All sizes.

FOR THOSE LEARNING DANCING.

1 Black Crêpe Dancing Tunic.

Lengths :	24″	26″	28″	30″	32″	34″	36″	38″	40″
	16/-	16/6	17/-	17/6	18/-	18/6	19/-	19/6	20/-

1 Pair Knickers to match.

Sizes :	14″	16″	18″	20″	22″	24″
	6/-	6/3	6/6	6/9	7/-	7/3

minute instructions about *standing* for the choir's anthem but *sitting* for the elocutionary rendering by Form Four. Since school songs seem often to have been set to music calculated to strain the adolescent voice to breaking point, the song usually needed rehearsing, too. Yet when, after all the preparation, the fuss, and the chivvying, the whole school broke into the school song, it was not to be forgotten. It was a moment which even school rebels remember in retrospect with an odd affection, and which makes them agree with Sir Henry Newbolt when he wrote:

> For, working days or holidays,
> And glad or melancholy days,
> They were great days and jolly days
> At the best School of all.

The school choir of Dick Sheppard School, Lambeth, practising for Speech Day in 1955.

Indeed, so well did the baronet-poet sum up the sentiment, that schools like the Blyth Secondary in Norfolk and the Streatham County Grammar School used his poem for their song. Sentimental it was, but sung by hundreds of girlish voices it seemed strangely right.

Schoolgirls of Blyth Secondary School on parade for Field Day, 1936.

The old programmes for these days take one back to that ordered world. On June 30th, 1958, Winterstoke Secondary Girls' School at Weston-super-Mare started off the big occasion with the school song:

> From the sea to the crest of the Mendips,
> To the Hundred of Winterstoke,
> Our land is full of the glory,
> Of our fine and ancient folk.
> A thousand years have swept o'er it,
> And proudly now we claim,
> The heritage of our fathers—
> And ancient and honoured name.

Then came the chairman's remarks, the headmistress's report, the presentation of certificates, the address, the votes of thanks. The school choir sang three songs including "O Waly, Waly" and "Time, You Old Gipsy Man" and there followed "verse speaking" which included the inevitable "Tarantella" by Hilaire Belloc. The crashing crescendos and whispered diminuendos, conducted by the elocution mistress, rounded off the day. That was Winterstoke, but with only a few minor variations the speech day mixture was (and possibly still is) repeated all over the country.

Speech Day was always a solemn occasion, a proper moment for the uplifting of the human spirit. Songs, therefore, that were suitable for Speech Day were usually ones that had a suitably inspiring verse. Before the war, the girls of the Abbey School, dressed in their white jap silk, sang with serious attention:

> As in the Abbey through the years
> The torch of faith was burning,
> So in the School that bears its name
> The radiance from that sacred flame
> Should light the ways of learning.

The big moment in 1934 for Elsie Lucas of the Royal Merchant Seamen's Orphanage. Lady Higgins presents her with the Debitt Prize for Good Influence, won by a popular vote among the girls.

It was a moment to recollect the school's foundation and so at Lawnswood High School, Leeds, the song, written by Mrs. Constance Dove to celebrate the school's hundredth birthday, brought to mind the pupils and staff of the past.

> For those who served in days long gone,
> Who brought to work a youthful zest,
> Who gave themselves with cheerful heart
> Unstintingly, nor sought for rest
> Until the firm resolve in every breast
> Beat high to seek the best,
> We praise Thy name, O Lord.

Speech Day and other celebrations were also the occasion for feelings of nostalgia, particularly from old girls. The Greycoat Hospital, Westminster, had a particularly nostalgic song. The last two verses were more than a little appropriate. One of the many old girls who recalled them for me was Mrs. Betty James who had been at school in 1918. More than half a century later she could still remember:

> There are golden days we shall never forget,
> And things to recall with a pang of regret,
> The lessons we've mastered, the matches we've won,
> The work we've completed or only begun.
>
> We shall think of it all in a far distant day,
> The friends that we love, our work and our play.
> We pray for the Present, we thank for the Past,
> The Future shall see its perfection at last.

Lawnswood High School girls line the route so as not to miss the very important person, HRH Prince George Duke of Kent, at the opening of new buildings in 1932.

Occasionally a school song is nostalgia from start to finish, like the song of Godolphin School, Salisbury. Written by its first modern headmistress, Miss Mary Douglas, the song seems to have been used at Commem, an old girls' day at the school.

> We remember the grounds, the gardens and flowers,
> The sweep of the downs and their shadow,
> The ride of the clouds and the singing of birds,
> The sunset on stream and on meadow.
> We remember the cricket and tennis and "lax"
> The captains who always were saying;
> "Now pull up the standard and don't think of self,
> But of House and of School and good playing."

Songs like this were ideal for reunions, and indeed many songs seem to mention both past, present and future pupils in the same verses, consciously trying to create a sense of the three memberships linked in the same school. At Uplands School, Poole, the song's last verse ended:

> Though the arm that forged is weakened,
> Still the links retain their hold
> And the younger children listen
> To the voices of the old.

At the Kendrick School, Reading, the final verse of the song reminded current pupils:

> Some have passed ahead on Life's highway,
> Some with us a little longer stay,
> All for blessings on our school will pray
> And join the Kendrick song.
> Floreat Kendricka! Floreat Kendricka!
> Floreat Kendricka!
> Long may our Lion roar!

At Caldecote Towers, Miss Medina Griffiths wrote a school song which, perhaps to make old girls feel welcome, specifically mentioned their presence.

> Ho! you who once were workers here,
> We bid you welcome true,
> And hail your presence as a sign
> Of friendly interest due:
> And "Memor and Fidelis" sing
> As side by side we stand,
> Once more in dear old Caldecote
> A friendly happy band.

A traditional Speech-Day programme with song, speeches, prizes, and a vote of thanks by the headgirl all listed in their place.

KENDRICK SCHOOL
SPEECH DAY

29th November, 1961

Programme

SCHOOL SONG: "Floreat Kendrica"   *P. R. Scrivener*

Our good founders lived in former days
'Tis to them we raise our song of praise;
Comrades all your hearts and voices raise
and sing the Kendrick Song.
Floreat Kendrica
Floreat Kendrica
Floreat Kendrica
Long may our Lion roar.

Kendrick is the name we all revere,
John and Mary to our hearts are dear;
Old companions come from far and near
and join the Kendrick Song.
Floreat Kendrica, etc.

Some have passed ahead on life's highway,
Some with us a little longer stay;
All for blessing on our School will pray
and join the Kendrick Song.
Floreat Kendrica, etc.

OPENING BY THE CHAIRMAN
MRS. M. K. LOGAN DAHNE, B.A.

THE HEAD MISTRESS'S REPORT

PRESENTATION OF PRIZES BY
MISS HILDA HARDING,
Manager of Barclays Bank, Hanover Street, London, W.1.

ORGAN SOLO: " An Easter Alleluia "   *Gordon Slater*
ELIZABETH BUTTON

ADDRESS
VOTE OF THANKS BY THE HEAD GIRL

The National Anthem

Old girls were a visible sign, not only that a school was building up a loyal clientele who would one day wish to send their own daughters to be educated there, but also of time passing. And Time is quite often hurrying near in school songs. Perhaps because the songs are so often written by adult schoolmistresses, they are conscious of girlhood's hours rapidly disappearing. In Southport, for instance, the girls of Brentwood School used to sing:

> The Brentwood girls of the days long ago
> Have left brave records of fame behind.
> Oh, will our names be remembered so,
> When our places here we have sadly resigned.
>
> *Chorus*
> Work while we work; play while we play;
> Patience and pluck will carry the day.
> Quickly our schooldays are slipping away,
> Quickly our schooldays are slipping away.

The same emphasis is found in the song of Canaan Park, an Edinburgh private school. Before the war, the schoolgirls, most of them little knowing how fast time passes, used to sing:

> Schooldays fly past all too soon and we scatter
> Knowing not whither life's journey may end;
> But of this we are certain and naught else can matter;
> Canaanite everywhere always means friend.
> For whether we turn in our playtime
> To racquet, mallet or ball,
> We have this for our guide, whatever betide,
> "Not for oneself but for all."

A Midsummer-Night's Dream *under the cedars of Parkfields Cedars School, Derby in 1949. Pretty fairies and swashbuckling elves.*

Over and over again the school songs attempt to console their singers for the passing of time. Friendships will last . . . the school will remain . . . or at least there is memory. Luton Girls' High School song had this verse:

> Let us tell again the memory
> In our happy song
> Of the roads we trod together,
> And the wonders that we found there,
> Where the ways of learning led us
> To the stars.

"The ways of learning" in the science laboratory of Putney County Secondary School around 1918.

And the girls of the Kilmorie Road School for Girls used to sing to the tune of "John Peel".

> When our schooldays end and we're far away,
> And we're out in the world at work or at play,
> In the toil and stress of the workaday,
> We will never forget Kilmorie.

"I can remember all this," wrote Mrs. Helena Kempson, "although I'm now sixty-seven years old. I'm happy to say I'm married to a Kilmorie boy, my one and only boyfriend in life." For some, at least, the romance of school is a real thing.

With the feeling that time was slipping by, came an ill-disguised apprehension. It's clear from some of the songs that the writers are uneasy about the world outside. The school is the best school of all, of course—but what when schooldays are over? Often the song is a fervent expression of hope that somehow, even after school, its principles will be a protecting influence. So the girls of Whitchurch High School, a school now amalgamated with the Sir John Talbot's Grammar School, used to sing:

Slowly across the Shropshire hills
The long cloud-shadows glide,
Where a great heart was laid to rest,
Our glory and our pride.
And if for us the shadows fall
And threatening clouds draw near,
We'll think how Talbot braved the foe
And face them without fear.

Among the Wycombe Abbey songs is one that echoes this apprehension. It was written in 1898 and is one of the earliest of the school's collection. *"In fide vade"* or "In faith go forward" is the school's motto.

In faith go forward! While our Mother Wycombe
Prepares us for the future none can tell!
In games and lessons, in our joys and sorrows,
These words must be our guide, will guide us well.

In faith go forward! Here we are forgotten,
Yet we forget not that we learnt from thee.
In life's great conflict, fought by each one singly,
Let us go forward, in faith, through faith, free.

Perhaps it was partly because of this apprehension that the leaving girls always cried on the last assembly, or the last chapel service of the term. Even the girls who wanted to leave, and the girls who had thought their weeping seniors "wet", cried. It was an experience so

Preparing for life with practice at the cricket nets of Caldecote Towers after the First World War.

universal that some schools had songs specially adapted for these heart-rending occasions. Clifton High School had a particularly emotional one which was sung on the last day of term as "Second Prayers". "Actually there was very little prayer," recalls Daphne Simon. "Most of the time was given to singing songs."

> One look back as we hurry o'er the plain,
> Many years speeding us along,
> One look back to the hollow past again,
> Youth comes flooding into song.
> Tell how once in the breath of Summer air
> Winds blew fresher than they blow;
> Times long hid with their triumph and their care,
> Yesterday, many years ago.

The leaving song for Newland High School, Kingston-upon-Hull, was equally romantic. The first headmistress, Miss Gertrude Rowland, decided in the 1920s that at the end of every year the leavers should have a song that they alone sung. The school had just moved to new buildings on the fringe of the city, surrounded by fields, with terraced gardens full of roses. Its motto was, and is, *"Ad Lucem"*, "Towards the Light". With these in mind Miss Rowland wrote this song for the girls who were leaving her:

> O, fair green fields beneath a wide spread heaven,
> O, leafy grove in whose cool shade I lie,
> O, flowery banks whereon the roses blossom,
> And rank on rank of colours greets the eye,
> I love you all, here stands, by you encircled,
> The School I love, the School whose face is set
> Towards the light, and urges me to follow,
> And may the time ne'er come when I its charge forget.

The love of school was the same, even when the sentiments were far less romantic. At the Clewer St. Stephen's School in Slough, the song was prosaic but the message was the same.

> If in the world a school one sought
> To guide and train the mind,
> The Clewer School where we are taught
> No better can one find.
>
> And when we leave, if 'tis our lot
> To mount an office stool,
> To teach or type, yet we will not forget
> Our dear old School.

For the girls of St. Leonards, the outlook was much jollier. "The Breaking-Up Song" was sung at a fast pace to the air of "Here's to the Maiden", and in 1891, the date of its composition, there was no mention of what the leavers might be going to do.

> Here's to the town on the grey northern shore,
> Here's to the School we believe in,
> Here's to the girls who are with us no more,
> And here's to the girls who are leaving.

> *Chorus*
> It's always the rule,
> Three cheers for the School!
> And three for the girls who are leaving!

At the Mount School, York, the leavers put on a special entertainment and a new song was written every year. The first one recorded in the school's songbook was for 1904 and it had a jolly chorus which went:

> Dear old school, though old scholars we may be,
> Good old school, present still our hearts with thee,
> Still our school, though we may be far from thee,
> With many a weary mile between.
> Goodbye—Goodbye.

In those days, it was possible to admit to sentiments that today would come in for mockery. So the 1907 leavers could sing:

The Caldecote Towers school orchestra in 1917, with headmistresses Miss Tate and Miss Tanner presiding on either side.

Sisterhood of many members,
Mount girls all, where'er they be,
Here tonight we sing thy praises,
Sing of what we owe to thee.
Though words fail in true expression,
Loyal are the thoughts below;
Thou, our school, our own "All-Mother"
Send thy blessing e'er we go.

Nowadays if loyalty to school, Queen and country is felt, it is not expressed. It would be positively bad manners to embarrass other people by doing so. So the present generation of schoolgirls at Pontefract and District High School would no doubt be embarrassed if asked to sing what used to be their school song during the war years. It is the quintessence of that old schoolgirl world that has gone for ever.

It isn't only lessons
We come to school to learn,
E'en here we know the changes
Of Fortune kind or stern.
We cannot all gain prizes
We can't win every game,
But though we're disappointed,
We love School just the same.

But one day we must leave it
And 'mid the world's stern strife
We'll know another teacher,
The great Headmistress Life.
Then may our old School's honour
Be still our proudest boast,
And may we e'er prove worthy
Of Her who taught us most.

Turning their backs on school: two young ladies of 1908 eager and ready to face the big wide world outside.

Photo Acknowledgments

I have to thank many people for the pictures. The *Sunday Times* and Topix provided illustrations on pages 15, 63, and 82 (also on the cover); the Greater London Photograph Library those on pages 37, 38, 42, 45 and 61; the Radio Times Hulton Picture Library those on pages 33, 49, 54, 57, 60, 65, 79, 113 and 115; Henry Grant one on page 64 and one inset on the cover; *The Age* newspaper, Melbourne, one on page 104; those on pages 99, 101, 102, 105, 106, 107 come from the Alexander Turnbill Library, Wellington, New Zealand; the photograph on page 125 is from the Mansell Collection.

Commercial firms helped me. The Educational Supply Association, Stevenage, provided the picture on page 41; Bentalls of Kingston-on-Thames those on pages 71 and 75; John Lewis Partnership's archives, Stevenage, those on pages 76, 77 and 80.

Schools were most kind. St. Bernard's, Westcliff-on-Sea, sent me their marvellous programmes; the Girls' Public Day School Trust lent me the drilling picture; the Convent of the Sacred Heart, Queen's Cross, Aberdeen, their photographs of early pupils; James Gillespie's High School, Edinburgh, their song sheet; Lawnswood School, Leeds, pictures on their first proper headmistress and the opening of new buildings.

The most marvellous finds were the pictures of Caldecote Towers which came from Max Hoather, Marjorie Steel and Doris Worssam. The cover photograph of the Bentley Friary girls and the Caldecote pictures on pages 32, 98 and 123 were taken by Max Hoather's father, W. Hoather. He probably took the others, too.

Pictures of Putney County Secondary School were lent by Jessie Horsnell; pictures of Blyth Secondary School by Beryl K. Rich; illustrations from Kendrick School and Wilton House School by Molly Chadwick; Parkfields Cedars pictures by Pem Gerard and Miss D. Stead; pictures from Howell's School by Sybil Tope; a photograph from King Edwards', Camp Hill, by Margaret Hewson; pictures from St. Monica's, Skipton, by Betty McEntegart; a picture of Queen's Cross by Alison MacKintosh; Hugh Walton lent me pictures from his mother's, Ethel Walton's, Queen's School, Margate. I am very grateful to them, and to all the other kind helpers whose pictures were lent but in the end did not appear in the book. One loan, in particular, moved me. Evelin Kerber not only lent me pictures, but also an amazing pair of hand-sewn pink gingham Skinners' School knickers. Alas, no picture could do them justice.

God and our du-ty is our call, Our best for each
Content with naught but on-ly best And in God's hand

Strive with the might of our fa-thers of old, Quae-ri-te